CONUNDRUM

ABOUT THE AUTHOR

Brian Clegg is the author of many books, including most recently *Professor Maxwell's Duplicitous Demon: The Life and Science of James Clerk Maxwell* (Icon, 2019) and *The Reality Frame: Relativity and Our Place in the Universe* (Icon, 2017). His *Dice World* and *A Brief History of Infinity* were both longlisted for the Royal Society Prize for Science Books. Brian has written for numerous publications including *The Wall Street Journal*, *Nature*, *BBC Focus*, *Physics World*, *The Times*, *The Observer*, *Good Housekeeping* and *Playboy*. He is the editor of popularscience.co.uk and blogs at brianclegg.blogspot.com.

www.brianclegg.net

CON

CRACK THE ULTIMATE

UND

CIPHER CHALLENGE!

RUM

BRIAN CLEGG

@BrianClegg
facebook.com/ConundrumBook
#ConundrumBook

Published in the UK in 2019
by Icon Books Ltd, Omnibus Business Centre,
39–41 North Road, London N7 9DP
email: info@iconbooks.com
www.iconbooks.com

Sold in the UK, Europe and Asia
by Faber & Faber Ltd, Bloomsbury House,
74–77 Great Russell Street,
London WC1B 3DA or their agents

Distributed in the UK, Europe and Asia
by Grantham Book Services,
Trent Road, Grantham NG31 7XQ

Distributed in the USA
by Publishers Group West,
1700 Fourth Street, Berkeley, CA 94710

Distributed in Australia and New Zealand
by Allen & Unwin Pty Ltd,
PO Box 8500, 83 Alexander Street,
Crows Nest, NSW 2065

Distributed in South Africa
by Jonathan Ball, Office B4, The District,
41 Sir Lowry Road, Woodstock 7925

Distributed in India by Penguin Books India,
7th Floor, Infinity Tower – C, DLF Cyber City,
Gurgaon 122002, Haryana

Distributed in Canada by Publishers Group Canada,
76 Stafford Street, Unit 300
Toronto, Ontario M6J 2S1

ISBN: 978-178578-410-1

Typeset in Sabon by Marie Doherty

Printed and bound in Great Britain
by Clays Ltd, Elcograf S.p.A.

For Gillian, Chelsea and Rebecca

ACKNOWLEDGEMENTS

Thanks to everyone at Icon Books who has helped make this the most enjoyable writing project I've ever been involved with. Particular thanks to Duncan Heath and Robert Sharman for editorial impact.

Contents

Getting Started

Welcome to *Conundrum*, a collection of cryptic puzzles in which the solutions build through the whole book to provide a single, solved conundrum. No answers are provided, but nearly all the puzzles in the first sixteen levels have hints at the back of the book in case you are struggling. After that, you are on you own. At the end of the sections are 'guardian' checkpoints which can only be solved with key words, letters or numbers produced during that section. This means that you can be assured that your answers are correct and complete to this stage before moving on to the next section.

There are twenty themed levels, ranging from chemistry to history. Each level has ten puzzles to solve, plus the guardian to confirm that the level has been successfully completed. Elements from each level's solution will be required later. The twentieth guardian gives you the opportunity to present your completed solution online.

The first correct solution provided to us will be splashed on the www.ConundrumBook.com website. All subsequent correct solvers will be listed in the Hall of Fame at www.ConundrumBook.com and, subject to deadline, will have the option of taking on a secondary 'expert puzzle' to be the next highlighted winner.

The puzzles in *Conundrum* often involve dealing with ciphers – if you aren't familiar with these, take a look at the Cracker's Guide in the next section.

The puzzles will end with a box for you to enter a level key character, number or word. These will be used to pass the end of level guardian.

Finally, a note about notes. You may have been brought up not to write in books – this isn't that kind of book. It's a good idea to write on the pages, particularly to keep a note of these level key characters. If you are using the e-book version you will need to either keep a notebook (physical or electronic) to jot down your solutions or use the note-making facility of your e-book reader if it provides one. Either way, I'd suggest having some paper and a pen or pencil on hand to play around with ideas and solutions.

Let's get cracking ...

Cracker's Guide

Here's a quick introduction to some forms of code and cipher. Strictly, a code represents a word or phrase by using a totally unconnected word – so, for example, FROG could mean 'buy $10,000 of Apple shares' – whereas a cipher typically substitutes characters in a message with other characters according to a set of rules. If you're familiar with cipher work, you can go straight to the first level.

Simple shift

Sometimes called a Caesar cipher, this is the most basic approach you can take to encrypting information. It's a form of substitution cipher, where one letter is substituted for another. It's simply a matter of shifting the alphabet by a specified number of letters. Like many ciphers, it's often best to draw up a table to help encipher and decipher a message. Let's say your shift was four letters – then we would have this table:

```
A B C D E F G H I J K L M N O P Q R S T U V W X Y Z
E F G H I J K L M N O P Q R S T U V W X Y Z A B C D
```

To encipher the message HELLO WORLD, we just look up each letter in the message in the top line and replace it with the letter from the bottom line. So, our message becomes LIPPS ASVPH.

Notice that the same letter always produces the same cipher character. This makes this technique susceptible to simple guesswork, particularly if the characters aren't grouped (see below, page xiv). The cipher is also easily broken if the message is long enough, by looking out for repetition of frequently used letters. In English, the frequency with which letters appear is roughly in the order ETAOINSHRDLCUMWFGYPBVKJXQZ going from E, the most common, to Z, the least. So, if you see X occurring very frequently, it may well represent an E, a T or an A.

Random substitution

One immediate way to make a substitution cipher like the simple shift a little trickier to crack is to shuffle up the replacement letters A–Z into a random order. This approach is still susceptible to using frequencies of letters, but it does mean that once you've got one letter right you don't automatically get the rest.

Sequence shift

Still simple to use, but significantly harder to spot, a sequence shift moves each letter of the message on by a number – but that number changes for every character, using a simple mathematical sequence. For example, you could use the odd numbers: 1, 3, 5, 7 ... To create your enciphered text just add these to each of the letters in the message. In all cipher work, 'adding a number' means moving on that number of spaces through the alphabet. So, for example:

```
H E L L O +
1 3 5 7 9
```

gives

```
I H Q S X
```

Note that L become Q the first time, but S the second time. If the addition takes you past the end of the alphabet, just loop around, following Z with A etc. To decipher the cipher text, subtract the number in the sequence from the letter, moving backwards down the alphabet.

It's possible that the number you add to encipher or subtract to decipher will be bigger than 26, in which case you have to go around the alphabet more than once. A simple way to get round this is go through the sequence and subtract 26 from any number bigger than 26. Repeat this until no number is bigger than 26 – you now have a simple number to deal with. So, for example, if your sequence was the squares:

1, 4, 9, 16, 25, 36, 49, 64 ...

a first pass subtracting 26 from numbers bigger than 26 gives:

1, 4, 9, 16, 25, 10, 23, 38 ...

and a second pass:

1, 4, 9, 16, 25, 10, 23, 12 ...

which you can now use to add (encrypt) or subtract (decrypt).

Going beyond letters

For simplicity, most of the ciphers in this book work only with the letters A to Z. However, any of the techniques described here could also include other characters – numbers or punctuation – simply by adding them to the end of the list of characters which will be manipulated. So, for example, if the letters are characters 1 to 26, we could then continue with the numbers 1 to 9, then 0 as characters 27 to 36. Once we have this list, it can be manipulated using any of the cipher techniques noted here.

Introducing other characters in this manner can make decryption harder. Just including the numbers, for example, it would be possible to add them before the letters, after the letters or interlaced with the letters. Similarly we could put 0 at the start of the numbers or at the end. So, for example we could work with:

```
ABCDEFGHIJKLMNOPQRSTUVWXYZ1234567890
1234567890ABCDEFGHIJKLMNOPQRSTUVWXYZ
ABCDEFGHIJKLMNOPQRSTUVWXYZ0123456789
0123456789ABCDEFGHIJKLMNOPQRSTUVWXYZ
A1B2C3D4E5F6G7H8I9J0KLMNOPQRSTUVWXYZ
```

... or any other way of mingling the letters and numbers, while the set of characters to generate the cipher could equally have letters and numbers mixed in any way.

Another way to add complexity is to introduce null characters that have no meaning and have to be ignored. This was one of the earliest ways used to strengthen simple substitution ciphers.

Grouping

Imagine you encipher the message I WANT YOU TO PUT THE BIG CUP INTO THE SMALL BOX using the shift cipher on page xi. The result is M AERX CSY XS TYX XLI FMK GYT MRXS XLI WQEPP FSB.

If we are trying to use letter frequencies to decrypt the message, this isn't a great text as its most common letters are T (six of them) and O (four), beating E, A, R and I. However, the way the cipher is broken up gives a lot away. We have M standing on its own – that is only likely to be an A or an I. We have the three-letter word XLI twice – an obvious thing to try here is THE. And we have the two-letter word XS – again, there are a limited number of common two-letter words.

To make the cipher a bit harder to crack, it's common to group the letters in, for example, blocks of five or as a single long string. This would make the cipher MAERX CSYXS TYXXL IFMKG YTMRX SXLIW QEPPF SB or MAERXCSYXSTYXXLIFMKGYTMRXSXLIWQEPPFSB. That way, less is given away. When this is deciphered the result is IWANT YOUTO PUTTH EBIGC UPINT OTHES MALLB OX or IWANTYOUTOPUTTHEBIGCUPINTOTHESMALLBOX – it's not as convenient to read as the original, but it is usually easy to work out what it means.

Transposition ciphers

An alternative to substitution is transposition, where all the characters from the plain text are still present, but the cipher process applies a rule to change their order, scrambling the message. One of the simplest is the rail fence cipher, where the message is broken into two or more lines and the enciphered text is produced by reading one character off each line in turn. So, for instance, using the simplest two-line rail fence we would break up:

```
PASSWORDTODAYISFRED
```

Into two lines, splitting them as near as possible to halfway:

```
PASSWORDTO
DAYISFRED
```

Then read off alternating lines to get:

```
PDAASYSIWSOFRRDETDO
```

The rule for rearranging the text can be as complex as you like. As the letters fit expected frequency patterns, after eliminating substitution ciphers, transposition is often the next possibility to try. Of course, it is also possible to combine the two, using a substitution cipher and then transposing the results.

Key ciphers

The most commonly used types of modern cipher involve one or more keys. This is a more sophisticated version of the sequence shift. There is a different value added to each letter, so it's a lot harder to crack than a simple shift, but here the amount each character is shifted varies according to a separate key, so there is no pattern as in the case of the sequence shift.

Ideally, the key should be a set of random characters and as long as the text to be enciphered. Meeting these conditions makes the cipher impossible to crack as the enciphered text has no pattern – but that means having to provide a key to each end of the communication link, which could be intercepted. For this reason, the key used is often something more memorable or easily obtained – but that does open up the possibility of cracking the cipher.

Commonly, the key is a word or phrase. If it's shorter than the message, the key is just repeated. So, for example if we used the key ENIGMA to encipher a message it would work like this:

Plain text:	MEETMEATFIVEPM
Key:	ENIGMAENIGMAEN
Cipher text:	RSNAZFFHOPIFUA

A common principle of cipher work is that letters are given a value based on their position in the alphabet: A=1, B=2 and so on. Here, to get to the cipher text, we add the value of each letter in the key to the plain text character. So, for example, E is 5, so we add 5 to the M in the original message, turning it into R. As before, if the addition takes you past Z, the alphabet simply restarts – subtract 26 (more than once if necessary) until you have a number that falls within the alphabet.

To decipher a message using a key, simply take the value of each letter in the key away from the value of the cipher text. So, in the above example, the first letter of the cipher text is R – we take away E (5), the first letter of the key, and get M.

If you are familiar with Excel, you will find a spreadsheet at www.ConundrumBook.com which will make it easy to quickly use key-based ciphers, doing the number crunching for you.

Book ciphers

A book cipher is probably more strictly a code, as the mechanism involves looking up words or letters in a table. Sender and receiver agree on a book to use as the source – each has a copy of the book. (It's essential they have the same edition.) The sender then looks up the words or characters they want to convey in the book and simply sends the positions of those words or letters. So, for instance, 16/03/08 could be word 8 on line 3 of page 16 – which also has the advantage of looking like a date. This is impossible to crack unless you know the book being used. The potential weak point in the system is the way that the choice is communicated between sender and receiver.

Array ciphers

An array cipher (my terminology) uses a table of text to provide the encryption. The most basic form is to write your message along the rows of a square table, filling any blanks with extra characters. Then you can rotate the table through 90 degrees by reading off columns. (This is just a different way of operating a rail fence cipher.) For example if I write my message WHAT TIME IS THE GAME TONIGHT without spaces and using Z as a filler in a 5 by 5 table I get:

W	H	A	T	T
I	M	E	I	S
T	H	E	G	A
M	E	T	O	N
I	G	H	T	Z

I can then read down the columns, one after another, to produce:

WITMIHMHEGAEETHTIGOTTSANZ

A more sophisticated approach puts a keyword in an extra row at the top of the table, then rearranges the columns to the alphabetic order of the letters in the keyword. So, if the keyword were SNAKE, we would rearrange the columns of the message in the order AEKNS. The encrypted message is then read off the columns of the table. The recipient needs to know the keyword to decipher the message. Here's the same message in such a table:

S	N	A	K	E
W	H	A	T	T
I	M	E	I	S
T	H	E	G	A
M	E	T	O	N
I	G	H	T	Z

The message is once again read off down the columns (ignoring the shaded cells) in the order AEKNS:

AEETHTSANZTIGOTHMHEGWITMI

An alternative substitution cipher using an array is to put the letters of the alphabet in a 5 × 5 table, then put two keywords along the top row and a left hand column. As there are 26 letters in the alphabet we need to allow one cell to stand for two of the letters. Most commonly, the same value is used for I and J (sometimes called I=J), for S and Z (S=Z) or for U and V (U=V). The result is something like this:

Key 2 / Key 1	S	N	A	K	E
B	A	B	C	D	E
L	F	G	H	I/J	K
I	L	M	N	O	P
M	Q	R	S	T	U
P	V	W	X	Y	Z

The alphabet can be in order, as here, or randomised (though if the latter, the sender and recipient have to share that structure, risking interception). To encipher a character, we look it up in the body of the table and note the letter from key 1 and key 2 corresponding to its row and column. Each letter in the plain text then becomes two letters in the cipher. So

PEEL

becomes

IEBEBEIS

If someone intercepting the cipher suspects it uses pairs of letters in this way, it becomes relatively easy to crack as it's just a substitution cipher where each letter pair is considered as a single letter, but otherwise it appears more confusing.

A more sophisticated array cipher is the Playfair cipher. For this, you set up a 5 × 5 table with all the letters (either I=J, S=Z or U=V). The grid is populated by using a memorable phrase, only ever using a letter from the phrase once, then filling in any gaps with the remaining letters of the alphabet. Here's a simple example, using the phrase 'Richard of York gave battle in vain.'

R	I/J	C	H	A
D	O	F	Y	K
G	V	E	B	T
L	N	M	P	Q
S	U	W	X	Z

To encipher we split the plain text into pairs of letters. If there's an odd number of characters in the message, stick an X or other random letter on the end. If two letters in a pair are the same, put an X in between them. We then look up the cipher by taking pairs as follows:

1. Find the letter at the intersection of the row of the first letter and the column of the second letter – this replaces the first letter in the pair
2. Find the letter at the intersection of the row of the second letter and the column of the first letter – this replaces the second letter in the pair.

If the letters are both on the same row, select the letter to the right of each letter. If the letters are in the same column, select the letter below each letter. If you're at the edge of the table, 'to the right' becomes the first letter in the same row and 'below' becomes the first letter in the same column.

So, for HAPPIEST we use HA PX PI ES and TX. Because H and A are in the same row, we take the letter to the right in each case. So H becomes A. Because A is in the rightmost column we wrap around to the start and A becomes R. P and X are in the same column. This means P becomes X, and X becomes H. P and I are not in the same row or column. So P becomes N, and I becomes H. Similarly, E becomes G, and S becomes W. Finally, T becomes B, and X becomes Z.

So HAPPIEST becomes ARXHNHGWBZ.

When deciphering, we use exactly the same process as enciphering for pairs that don't share rows or columns, but where the letters are in the same row or same column, the shift is in the opposite direction.

There are far more sophisticated array ciphers, such as the Vigenère cipher, where we typically have a 26 by 26 grid with each row the whole alphabet, shifted one each time. We then add a top row and left-hand column containing the whole alphabet again. This is combined with a keyword, used as in the key ciphers section. To encipher the text, we find the first letter of the plain text as the column and the first letter of the keyword as the row and look up the value in the 26 × 26 table. This makes for a significantly more complex arrangement.

There are computer mechanisms to crack this type of cipher, particularly if the keyword repeats and there is repeated text in the message. However, it is arguably beyond most pen and paper cracking, so we have not used Vigenère ciphers or more sophisticated variants in this book.

More ciphers and codes

We can only give a brief introduction here. You can find a fair amount of information on Wikipedia regarding ciphers and codes, but if you find the topic interesting, here are three book recommendations to find out more:

The Code Book, Simon Singh (Fourth Estate, 1999) – a very readable history of the development of codes and ciphers from ancient Greece to the twentieth century.

De/Cipher, Mark Frary (Modern Books, 2017) – an easy-to-read introduction to codes, ciphers and code-breaking techniques through history, including a few unbroken mysteries.

Unsolved!, Craig Bauer (Princeton University Press, 2017) – more heavyweight reading, but still very interesting. Each chapter focuses on an unsolved piece of cryptic writing from the Voynich Manuscript through the Zodiac Killer letters to the CIA's Kryptos sculpture. As he goes, Bauer introduces different code and cipher techniques from the most basic to modern electronic forms.

The Puzzles

LEVEL 1 - LITERATURE

1. Caesar's novel

Decrypt the title of this well-known novel:

```
YMJ HFYHMJW NS YMJ WDJ
```

Level key character 1: fourth letter of the decrypted solution

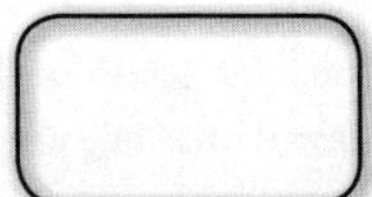

2. Literary numeracy

Add together the number of towers in the second book of the *Lord of the Rings* to Agatha Christie's *Little Indians*, Alison Weir (or Antonia Fraser)'s *Wives of Henry VIII*, T.E. Lawrence's *Pillars of Wisdom* and John Buchan's *Steps*.

Take the square root of the total to find the number that is **level key character 10**:

3. The spy's library

The security services have discovered that a spy is using a collection of books as a clever way of passing on a message. He sets up a number of books in a position visible from a window and his contact uses the books' spines to receive a message. He has recently passed on the time of a meeting to his contact, using this set of books:

The security services know that to keep things simple, he is using the same positioned letter from the same piece of information on each book spine to communicate one letter of the message. What time is the meeting?

Level key character 5: third letter of the decrypted solution

4. A useful title

… And What Alice Found There.

Source:
T O M A T O

Encrypt this source as instructed by the title:

Level key character 2: fifth letter of the encrypted solution

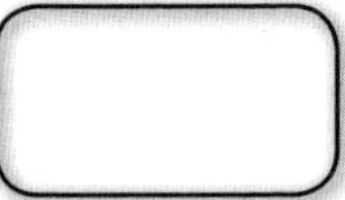

5. Pulitzer puzzle

These books have all won the Pulitzer Prize for Fiction. Which other Pulitzer-winning title, whose author rejected the prize, does the list also mention?

A Fable (William Faulkner)
Rabbis and Wives (Chaim Grade)
Roots (Alex Haley)
One of Ours (Willa Cather)
Where I'm Calling From (Raymond Carver)
Scarlet Sister Mary (Julia Peterkin)
Mean Spirit (Linda Hogan)
I Wish This War Were Over (Diana O'Hehir)
To Kill a Mockingbird (Harper Lee)
Honey in the Horn (Harold L. Davis)

Level key character 7: ninth letter of the solution

6. Lost in Austen

Which Jane Austen character's surname has been used as the key to encrypt *Pride and Prejudice* here?

TSAGD EOV SQIKMGHGF

Level key character 6: second letter of the solution

7. What the Dickens?

Here are some of Charles Dickens' many novels, with their year of publication:

A Tale of Two Cities – 1859
Bleak House – 1853
David Copperfield – 1850
Great Expectations – 1861
Martin Chuzzlewit – 1844
Oliver Twist – 1839
The Pickwick Papers – 1837

To find our key character, put these Dickens characters in chronological order of the novel they appeared in: Magwitch, Bumble, Pecksniff, Manette, Weller.

Level key character 8: second letter of the name of the second character in chronological order.

8. Genesis

You wouldn't expect a literary level without a book cipher. Let's start the way that King James VI of Scotland would have liked the very beginning. Decipher this:

LZYDJTPPWU

Level key character 4: last letter of the decrypted solution

9. Spot the pastiche

The science fiction writer John Sladek wrote a series of pastiches of other science fiction writers' work (collected in his book *The Steam-Driven Boy*). Your task is to guess from the author and title of three of Sladek's stories which author from the 'golden age' of science fiction is being gently mocked:

Broot Force by Iclick-as-I-Move
Engineer to the Gods by Hitler I.E. Bonner
Joy Ride by Barry duBray

Level key character 3: Take the first letter of the second author's first name. Move back in the alphabet by the number value of the last letter of the first author's first name. Move back in the alphabet by the number value of the third letter of the final author's surname.

10. Decoding the rose

The final phrase of Umberto Eco's novel *The Name of the Rose* begins 'stat rosa pristina nomine', which roughly translates as 'the old rose remains only in name' – clearly linked to the name of the novel, though it's not clear whether the novel is named for the quote or the quote was used because of the name of the novel. It is a quote from the medieval Bernard of Cluny. However, the version Eco used was probably a bad copy where a letter in the word 'rosa' was incorrect.

Given that the text before in Bernard's poem is 'Nunc ubi Regulus aut ubi Romulus aut ubi Remus', what should the second word of Eco's quote probably be?

Level key character 9: take the letter replacing the incorrect letter and move back one in the alphabet.

LITERATURE - End of Level Guardian

You should now have ten characters from the ten puzzles. Slot them into this table:

1	2	3	4	5	6	7	8	9	10

If you've got all ten correct you should be able (allowing for a touch of textspeak) to do this to yourself. If the guardian word doesn't make any sense, you've got at least one of the puzzles wrong – check them.

If the guardian word makes sense, you are nearly ready to move on to the next level. You just need to find a key number, which will be used later. Add together the numerical value of each of the characters 1–9 in the guardian word.* Add on the actual number that is the tenth character. Subtract 100. Note down this number as the Level 1 key.

* Shortcut: If you're using the online spreadsheet, just type the first nine characters of the guardian word into the plain text row of the top, ENCRYPT section. For the 10th character use the letter with character 10 as its number value. The sum will be shown under AUTOSUM further down the first column.

Level 1 Key Number

LEVEL 2 - GEOGRAPHY

1. An L of a country

What is the capital of the only country whose name begins with L and has 13 letters?

Level key character 9: fourth letter of the capital's name.

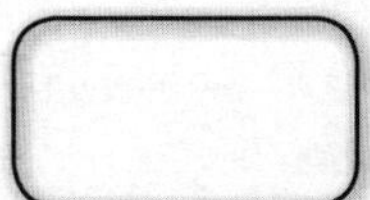

2. Forecasting the name

What is missing from the gap in this list?

… FitzRoy, Sole, Lundy, Fastnet, Irish Sea, Shannon, Rockall, ?, Hebrides, Bailey …

Level key character 3: fourth letter of the missing word

3. Filling the gap

Canada–Ambassador–USA

Bulgaria–New Europe–Romania

Israel–Allenby–Jordan

Denmark–?–Sweden

Level key character 10: second letter of the missing word

4. The secret city

Our code experts have intercepted a message they know refers to a European city, which at first sight seems to be a language out of *Star Wars*:

GUGICO BUGO GUBU

Noticing the regular pattern of consonant/vowel, they guess that this is an array cipher (see page xix) made by setting up a grid of the alphabet and reading off a consonant and vowel to represent the letter. From previous cracked messages, they know that the grid letters are in alphabetic order (omitting Z) and know the position of the letters D and T in the cipher column. So, if you wanted to encipher 'LOW' you would find L in the main grid and represent that by DE, O as DU and W as TI – the enciphered message would be DEDUTI.

	A	E	I	O	U
	A	B	C	D	E
	F	G	H	I	J
D	K	L	M	N	O
	P	Q	R	S	T
T	U	V	W	X	Y

Decipher the city.

Level key character 1: sixth letter of the city's name.

5. Numeric ties

If 4427 takes you from the UK to South Africa, 146 from USA to Sweden and 4953 from Germany to Cuba, how will 3391 route you?

Level key character 7: first letter of the first country in 3391.

6. Heading East

?, Zambia, Malawi, Mozambique

Morocco, ?, Tunisia, Libya, Egypt

Namibia, ?, Zimbabwe, Mozambique

Mauritania, Mali, Niger, ?, Sudan, Eritrea

Cameroon, Central African Republic, South Sudan, ?, Somalia

Level key character 2: Take the initial letters of the missing countries as a sequence. Use the next letter in the sequence as the level key character

7. Above their station

The secret services have intercepted a spy's letter. It is apparently innocuous, but actually describes a four-stop railway journey that the recipient must make to collect hidden files. Work out which four UK towns or cities need to be visited:

> Dear Simon,
>
> Thanks for the recommendation: I have just finished reading Waverley – I was very impressed. As you know, I like my eggs Sunnyside up, but they have not been good lately. I blame that new Tanshelf cooker I bought last year. I might buy a new one, but I'll wait until after my boat trip – I'm sailing from Bank Quay this year.
>
> All the best,
>
> Sebastian

Level key character 8 should be the second letter of the second town. It's also the second letter of the third town and the penultimate letter of the fourth town.

8. A capital cipher

We have intercepted a short cipher message. Before it was sent, we received a string of country names in plain text, followed by the word 'CAPITALS'. They are clearly something to do with the cipher. Can you help decipher it?

AUSTRALIA, BOTSWANA, CANADA, DOMINICA, ECUADOR, FRANCE, GHANA, HONDURAS, INDONESIA, JAMAICA, KENYA, LEBANON, MONGOLIA, NAURU, OMAN, PAKISTAN, QATAR, REPUBLIC OF MACEDONIA, SIERRA LEONE, TRISTAN DE CUNHA, USA, VIETNAM, ZAMBIA. CAPITALS.

ZTHHTD GSHTD E

Level key character 4 is described by the cipher.

9. State of the nation

We have two US states in outline, State A:

and State B:

Subtract State B from State A, taking the number value of each letter of the state's abbreviation individually from the other. For example, taking California from Maine would mean ME – CA: we take the C from the M to get J and A from E to get D, producing JD.

Level key character 6: add the number values of the two letters produced together and take away one to get the number value of the character.

10. Zoning out

A foreign agency has devised an unusual way to conceal a message. They are using the internet to send each character of a short message from different parts of the world. But each time the character they send is K. The list of locations the message is sent from is: Kuwait, Uruguay, Alaska, France, Vanuatu and New Zealand.

The only clues we have to crack the code are that it involves time zones (Standard Time) and that the information provided somehow specifies how far to move through the alphabet from the previous letter, starting with K. So, for example, if you worked out that the first increment was 5 and the second increment was –2, then the first characters in the message are KPN, because P is 5 further on than K and N is 2 back from P.

Level key character 5 is the key given by the message.

GEOGRAPHY - End of Level Guardian

You should now have ten characters from the ten puzzles. Slot them into this table:

1	2	3	4	5	6	7	8	9	10

If you've got all ten correct, the guardian phrase tells you the Level 2 key. If the guardian phrase doesn't make any sense, you've got at least one of the puzzles wrong – check them. Note down the number as the Level 2 key.

Level 2 Key Number

LEVEL 3 - MOVIES

1. Don't quote me

'A boy's best friend is his mother.'

'Oh, no, it wasn't the airplanes. It was beauty killed the beast.'

'You talking to me?'

This strange conversation was overheard shortly before this enciphered message was sent:

VHTUBXXNGAHDDSOTMWI

It seems the conversation gives the key to decipher the text using a simple, text-only key cipher, but it's not the words used in the conversation that are the key.

Level key character 4: the result of the calculation in the message

2. Mangled marquee

It's 1977 (time machine provided). You head to the cinema to choose between two of the hot films of the year ... only some joker has rearranged the sign.

Which movies could you have seen?

Level key character 9: the numerical value of the second letter of the name of the film with an F in it.

3. Cine link

Which movie titles link the following:

Fritz Lang–?–*Superman*

Steven Spielberg–?–*The Spy Who Loved Me*

Use the second title as a (letters only) key to encrypt the first title.

Level key character 10: the number value of the antepenultimate letter of the encrypted result

4. Of all the bars

The classic movie *Casablanca* is set during wartime, when conveying secrets safely was particularly important. Casablanca is also an unusual word because of the number of times it features the letter A. Our codemaker, inspired by watching Humphrey Bogart and Ingrid Bergman, has designed a cipher which involves choosing a single letter which will appear repeatedly in the enciphered message. The message is simply found by extracting each of the letters that appears immediately *after* the repeated letter. Unfortunately, she didn't say what that repeated letter is.

Source:

I BET PEWS OR LEISURE CHAINS CAN SEEM TO STINK OF EFFORT, GEORGE, UNDER NO ILLUSIONS OF VANITY.

Level key character 8: given in the message

5. Oscar logic

If you add together the number of Academy Awards that Oscar winners *Forrest Gump*, *The Lord of the Rings: The Fellowship of the Ring* and *The Curious Case of Benjamin Button* received, you get the number of nominations each film had. The most nominations any film has received ever is fourteen – which is twice as many as the number of awards won by *Lord of the Rings* plus *Button*. Given *Gump* got twice as many awards as *Button* and *Lord of the Rings* one more than *Button*, how many awards did *Gump* get?

Level key character 2: the answer.

6. SciFi snooze

What might *Blade Runner*'s replicants dream of?

Level key character 6: number of the penultimate character of the first word of the answer.

7. Masked movie

The name of a classic movie is being used as a passphrase to gain access to a secret location. We've got an encrypted version of the name and we know it has been encrypted with a sequence substitution, adding a value from an increasing numerical sequence to each letter. The only other information we have are the words 'Prime mover'.

VKJTLTEBCLHPCKNFCNC

Level key character 5: you'll know the number when you've decrypted the message.

8. Movie maths

Take the number that flew over the cuckoo's nest from a space odyssey. Divide by days of summer. Multiply by slaughter-house and divide by your starter for.

Level key character 3: the final number.

9. Strange meeting

If a new Greek prefix, a Greek god of dreams and the first atomic bomb test are virtually together, where are we?

Level key character 1: number of letters in the answer (excluding any grammatical articles).

10. The Imitation Game

One of the greatest codebreakers in history (as well as a pioneer of computing) was Alan Turing, who was portrayed in the film *The Imitation Game*.

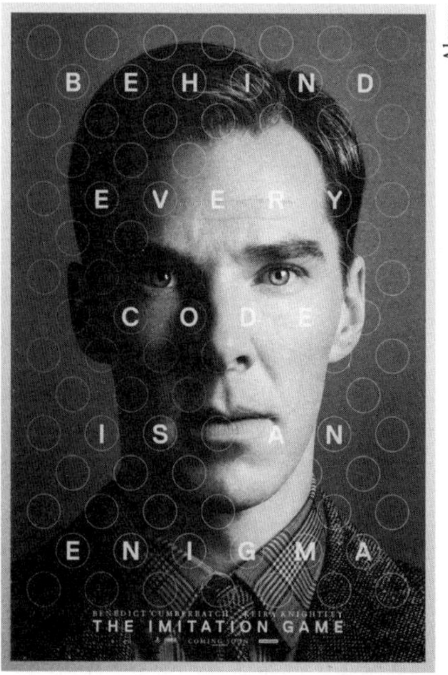

Alamy

A spy has had the bright idea of using the *Imitation Game* poster (above) as an encryption device. She has produced the message below. We know it was done by putting the plain code into the rows of circles immediately above text on the poster and adding or subtracting number values of the letters

Level key character 7: you'll know the number when you've decrypted the message.

in adjacent circles. Can you decrypt it? For clarity, we have extracted the grid and reproduced it below.

PXPCJHEXWXHY

This is our trickiest challenge yet: have a try before checking the hint.

MOVIES - End of Level Guardian

You should now have ten numbers from the ten puzzles. Slot them into this table:

1	2	3	4	5	6	7	8	9	10

Add up the numbers to get the Level 3 key.

Level 3 Key Number

It would be frustrating to get all the way through *Conundrum* and have one of your key numbers wrong, as you will need them all to crack puzzles in the final level. Here are two checks:

1. Add together the first three level keys. Add together the digits of the answer. If the result has more than one digit, add those digits together – repeat until you have a single digit. The answer should be 2. (E.g. if the sum of the first three level keys was 529, adding together the digits gives 5+2+9 = 16. This is more than one digit, so 1+6 =7, which would be the answer.)

2. Add together the individual digits of all three level keys. You should get 29.

LEVEL 4 - CHEMISTRY

1. Match the source

These chemical compounds all have natural sources, but which is which?

Chemical compound	**Source**
Aconite	*Aspergillus terreus*
Chymosin	Cinchona bark
Citral	Ruminant stomachs
Keratin	Human hair
Lovastatin	Lemongrass
Quinine	Meadowsweet
Salicylic acid	Wolf's bane

Level key word 8: first letter is first letter of the aconite source, second letter is penultimate letter of the compound from *Aspergillus terreus*, third letter is the third letter of compound from lemongrass and final letter is the fifth letter of the source of quinine.

2. Mendeleev's mystery

When Mendeleev first came up with his periodic table he predicted the existence of a number of unknown elements, giving them the name 'eka' (Sanskrit for the number 1) followed by the name of the element above them in the table – so 'ekasilicon' is the element below silicon, which eventually became germanium. A sneaky chemist has used his periodic table to encrypt a message. Each double digit in the encrypted value corresponds to an atomic number. These are the 'eka' values. So, find the actual numbers and turn them into letters.

36393232173215

Level key word 7: the result of this message

1	2	3	4	5	6	7	8	9	10	11	12	13	14	15	16	17	18
1 H																	2 He
3 Li	4 Be											5 B	6 C	7 N	8 O	9 F	10 Ne
11 Na	12 Mg											13 Al	14 Si	15 P	16 S	17 Cl	18 Ar
19 K	20 Ca	21 Sc	22 Ti	23 V	24 Cr	25 Mn	26 Fe	27 Co	28 Ni	29 Cu	30 Zn	31 Ga	32 Ge	33 As	34 Se	35 Br	36 Kr
37 Rb	38 Sr	39 Y	40 Zr	41 Nb	42 Mo	43 Tc	44 Ru	45 Rh	46 Pd	47 Ag	48 Cd	49 In	50 Sn	51 Sb	52 Te	53 I	54 Xe
55 Cs	56 Ba	*	72 Hf	73 Ta	74 W	75 Re	76 Os	77 Ir	78 Pt	79 Au	80 Hg	81 Tl	82 Pb	83 Bi	84 Po	85 At	86 Rn
73 Fr	74 Ra	**	104 Rf	105 Db	106 Sg	107 Bh	108 Hs	109 Mt	110 Ds	111 Rg	112 Cn	113 Uut	114 Fl	115 Uup	116 Lv	117 Uus	118 Uuo
	*	57 La	58 Ce	59 Pr	60 Nd	61 Pm	62 Sm	63 Eu	64 Gd	65 Tb	66 Dy	67 Ho	68 Er	69 Tm	70 Yb	71 Lu	
	**	89 Ac	90 Th	91 Pa	92 U	93 Np	94 Pu	95 Am	96 Cm	97 Bk	98 Cf	99 Es	100 Fm	101 Md	102 No	103 Lr	

3. The self-eating snake

German chemist Friedrich August Kekulé von Stradonitz (known more compactly as Kekulé) literally dreamed up the structure of the compound benzene. The ring structure came to him as snake-like chains of atoms danced around in a dream: 'But look! What was that? One of the snakes had seized hold of its own tail, and the form whirled mockingly before my eyes.'

A chemist had the cunning idea of using a set of benzene ring diagrams to encipher a message as:

LEI KEDYTS LVRWEF EOE

Here are his diagrams:

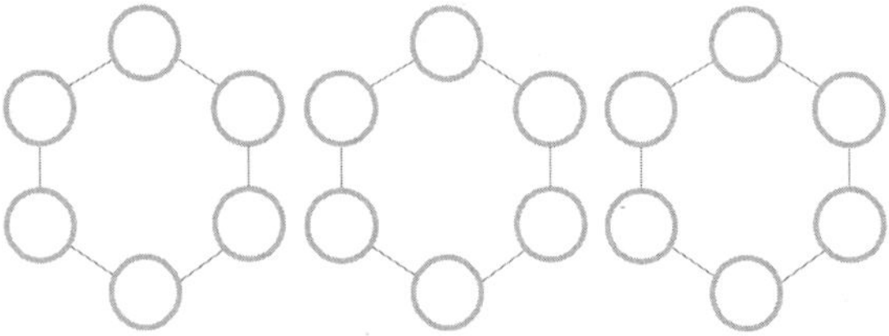

What did the message say?

Level key word 10: given in the deciphered text

4. Elementary

MI6 suspects a chemistry professor of espionage. He has sent the formula for a compound which is clearly a cryptic message – but what does it say?

NArHHe CPArAlScMgH CaPAlPArArPV

Level key word 6 is the last six letters of the decrypted message.

5. Discovery dates

These substances were discovered on the following dates: Before 1 BC, 1756, 1841, 1879, 1932, 1938, 1950 and 1952. But which date belongs to which substance?

Adamantane
Californium
Carbon dioxide
Einsteinium
PTFE
Saccharin
Theobromine
Zinc oxide

Level key word 3: first letter is first letter of oldest discovery, second letter is the fourth letter of the 1841 discovery, third letter is sixth letter of the 1950 discovery, final letter is the final letter of the most recent discovery.

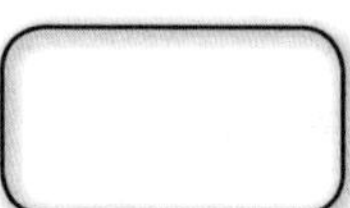

6. Furtive formulae

Another suspicious chemist (there seem to be a lot of them around) has left this chemical formula on the whiteboard. The trouble is, it doesn't make any sense as a reaction.

$$C_9H_{20} + Al_9O_{19} \rightarrow C_{15}O_{22} + Al_5H_{18}$$

Level key word 4 is given in the deciphered message.

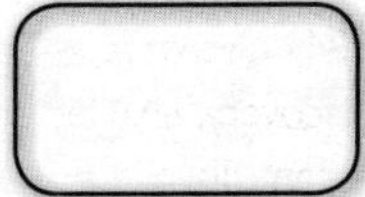

7. Ancient combinations

According to an alchemist, what we are looking for is in tin but not in iron, in helium but not in calcium or lead, in radium but not in radon or lanthanum, in sodium but not in rubidium or gold.

Level key word 5 spelled out here.

8. Canny compounds

Adamantium
Aragonite
Australium
Denatonium
Dilithium
Feminum
Kryptonite
Mythril
Phlogopite
Vibranium

Some of these compounds and minerals are real, some are fictional. But which are which?

Level key word 9: how many of these are real, written as a word.

9. Entangled elements

The periodic table has seven horizontal periods and eighteen vertical groups of elements. Which group number (omitting lanthanides and actinides) does this cryptic collection of letters refer to?

DMMMMNTV

Level key word 1: the group number as a word.

10. Chemist's crib

We've found the method used by a chemist to hide a message – we just need to rebuild her 'crib' or cheat sheet. The message is enciphered in pairs of characters. For the first character in a pair we read off the character below in the same column (wrapping round to the top of the same column if necessary). For the second character of the pair we read off the character to the right (wrapping round to the left of the row if necessary). To decrypt we reverse this – so first character of a pair, the decrypt is the character above and for the second character in a pair we read the character to the left.

We first need to fill in the crib. It was made by writing in left to right, filling one row at a time. The letters are from the names of the first nine chemical elements in order, but only adding unique letters – once a letter is already in the grid, we don't add it again. The remaining spaces are filled with the missing letters of the alphabet in order (without Z). Here's the cipher:

FYMD GXFN KXFV

Level key word 2 is the plural of the animal best known for this.

CHEMISTRY - End of Level Guardian

You should now have ten words from the ten puzzles. Write them in below:

1. ____
2. ____
3. ____
4. ____
5. ____
6. ____
7. ____
8. ____
9. ____
10. ____

The result should be a (rather silly, but comprehensible) sentence. The total number of letters in the sentence makes the key number.

Level 4 Key Number

LEVEL 5 - MUSIC

1. Elgar's enigma

The Enigma Variations was just one example of composer Edward Elgar's fondness for cryptography. He produced the 'Dorabella cipher' in a letter to Dora Penny, based on fractions and multiples of the letter E in his signature in different orientations, which is unbroken to this day. Here's a simpler substitution cipher using similar characters.

To decipher it you will need a table like this, filling in the missing symbols, then assign a letter to each of 24 symbols (X and Z are missing).

Loops/ Orientation	1	2	3	4	5	6
1						
2						
3						
4						

Level key character 4: given in the message

2. Prog (rock) nosis

21st Century Schizoid Man

And the Mouse Police Never Sleeps

Flight of the Snow Goose

I've Seen All Good People

The Return of the Giant Hogweed

Welcome to the Machine

Like or loathe the genre, you have to admire the oddity of some progressive rock song titles. Match the above titles with the correct bands in the list below.

1. Camel
2. Genesis
3. Jethro Tull
4. King Crimson
5. Pink Floyd
6. Yes

Level key character 6: With the list ordered alphabetically by band name, add the character number (i.e. A=1, B=2 etc.) of the final letter of the fourth song to the character number of the final letter of the penultimate song. That is the character number of the required letter.

3. Note the note

As soon as the musical notes were given standardised letters A to G, composers began to play with enciphering words into their music. Bach was famous for doing this and, making use of a German oddity, was even able to spell out his own surname. We've used Bach's cheat and taken the cheating one stage further, allowing an A to stand in for an O. All you have to do is select the appropriate picture for this word. (Note, some pictures are impossible to spell.)

Level key character 2: the letter accompanying the appropriate picture.

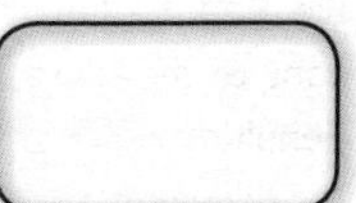

4. Keyboard capers

When MI6 searched a Russian spy's home they found that his piano had letters pencilled in on the keys. He had written out the alphabet repeatedly using all the keys, but only the white keys were legible. So the start looked like this:

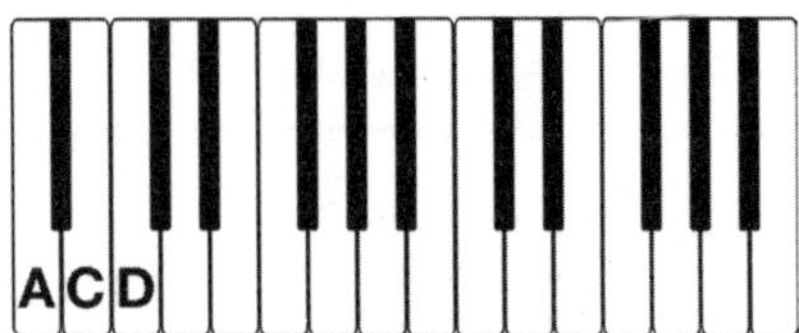

As there were 52 white keys, it seems likely that he was using an alternating substitution, using the first 26 letters on the keyboard for the first letter in the message, then the second 26 for the second letter in the message and so on. The spy would count along the 26 keys to the letter number of the plain text character, then write down the letter written on that key as the cipher text. The cipher doesn't produce unique values – but he was writing in English, so the context should be enough to guess the meaning. The complete keyboard is opposite.

And the cipher read:

IXH SW X

Level key character 10: spelled out in the cipher.

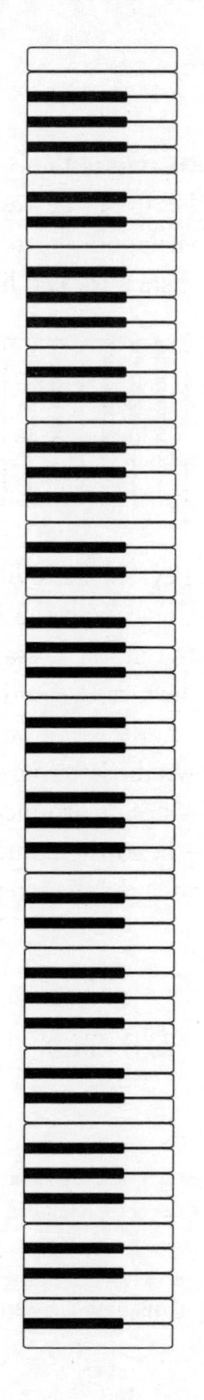

5. Colourful songs

________ Angel (Artiste: 'R. O.')

________ Disease (Artiste: 'P. J.')

________s for Your Furs (Artiste: 'B. H.')

Apples and ________s (Artiste: 'P. F.')

Goodbye ________ Brick Road (Artiste: 'E. J.')

Little ________ Rooster (Artiste: 'S. C.')

Mood ________ (Artiste: 'D. E.')

Sort the songs into the order of the rainbow colours, starting at red.

Level key character 1: after sorting, add the character number (i.e. A=1, B=2 etc.) of the antepenultimate letter of the last artiste's name to the character number of the final letter of the first word of the second artiste's name. This gives the character number of the required letter.

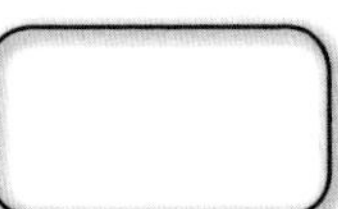

6. Melodic mystery

Decode the encrypted text using the words of this Christmas carol as the key.

Encrypted: `CTWPZ WWSJQ`

Level key character 5: detailed in the decryption.

7. Sung down under

National anthems are played at sporting events around the world, but we often struggle to remember the words. This is the first verse of the Australian national anthem, but one word is missing. Work out the missing word.

> Australians all let us rejoice,
> For we young and free;
> We've golden soil and wealth for toil;
> Our home is girt by sea;
> Our land abounds in nature's gifts
> Of beauty rich and rare;
> In history's page, let every stage
> Advance Australia Fair.
> In joyful strains then let us sing,
> Advance Australia Fair.

Level key character 8: what letter is suggested by the missing word?

8. Bootleg Beatles

This CD was sent through the post to a suspected spy with the note: 'Ignore "Favourite Beatles", numbers, spaces and punctuation.'

Favourite Beatles

1. Love Me Do
2. Being for the Benefit
3. Let It Be
4. September in the Rain
5. If I Fell
6. Mean Mr Mustard
7. Ob-La-Di, Ob-La-Da
8. Penny Lane
9. Can't Buy Me Love

We know that it identifies a letter by its position in the alphabet, essential to crack a cipher. But which letter?

Level key character 9: that letter.

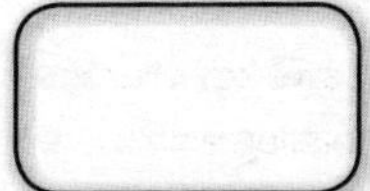

9. Symphonic sums

Subtract Mozart's 'Jupiter' from Haydn's 'London'. Divide by the sum of Beethoven's 'Eroica' and 'Pastoral'. Multiply by Vaughan Williams' 'Pastoral', and finally take away Mahler's 'Titan'.

Level key character 7: the letter corresponding to the outcome of the sum.

10. Disharmonic cipher

This (unpleasant) piece of music appears to be a cipher. The text below it has been captured in a raid:

Treble \ Bass	A	B	C	D	E	F	G
F	A	B	C	D	E	F	G
G	H	I	J	K	L	M	N
A	O	P	Q	R	S	T	U
B	V	W	X	Y	Z	1	2
C	3	4	5	6	7	8	9
D	Ø	£	$	&	@	%	.

Level key character 3: once deciphered you will know the letter

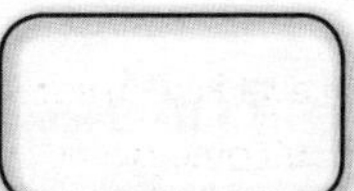

MUSIC - End of Level Guardian

You should now have ten characters from the ten puzzles. Slot them into this table:

1	2	3	4	5	6	7	8	9	10

If you've got all ten correct, the guardian word should make sense. If the guardian word doesn't make any sense, you've got at least one of the puzzles wrong – check them.

To work out the Level 5 key number add together the numeric values of all ten letters and divide by two. (Remember, if you're using the online spreadsheet, you can use it to do this addition – see page 15.)

Level 5 Key Number

LEVEL 6 - BIOLOGY

1. Botanic banter

There's nothing enthusiastic gardeners like better than baffling the rest of us with the Latin names of plants. Match the formal names to the common:

Common marigold	*Atropa belladonna*
Deadly nightshade	*Calendula officinalis*
Holly	*Ficus nemosis*
Mandrake	*Helianthus annuus*
Potato	*Ilex aquifolium*
Sunflower	*Mandragora officinarum*
Tousel	*Solanum tuberosum*

... but there is a catch. One of the plants (and its Latin equivalent) is made up.

Level key character 1: for the fictional plant, add the number of letters in the common name to the number of letters in the Latin (don't count spaces). If the result is bigger than 9, add the two digits together. Repeat if necessary until you have a single digit.

2. DNA Codons

The DNA code uses just four letters, representing the initials of the 'bases': A for adenine, C for cytosine, G for guanine and T for thymine. Bases occur in groups of three on genes, each group indicating one of the twenty different amino acids that can be made into proteins, or a control instruction.

A security agency has found a way to conceal messages in a portion of the DNA of a small organism, which can then be used to transfer the message undetected. You have sequenced the DNA (reproduced below) and now have to decode the message.

Source:

ATG ATG GAA GAG ACC ACG CGC GAG GTT ATA
TTT GTG AAT ACT GCC ATT AAC TTC ATC CGA TCC
ACA GAT GAG TGT TTT ATC GTT GAA CCC ATG TAA

Level key character 2: the hour of the meeting (number).

3. Genome storage

Genomes – the information stored in DNA – vary enormously in size between organisms. The size of the genome is measured in number of base pairs. The smallest known is around 1,800 base pairs and the largest at least 150 billion base pairs. If we could store one base pair in one byte, which is the smallest of these storage media we could use to hold the human genome? (If there isn't one big enough, use multiples of the largest.)

Floppy disk – 360 Kb
Diskette – 1.44 Mb
CD – 700 Mb
DVD – 4.7 Gb
Blu-Ray disc – 25 Gb
Memory stick – 64 Gb

Level key character 3: the capacity of the storage medium. If it has decimals, round up. If it's bigger than 9 add the digits together. Repeat if necessary until you have a single digit.

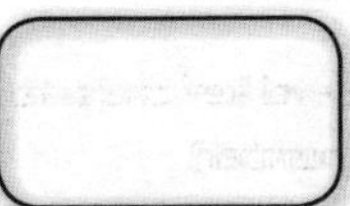

4. Textbook teaser

Opposite is a passage from an uncorrected proof copy of the book *Science for Life*. The author has incorporated a secret message into the text. (The message was removed before the final version of the book was printed.)

What does it say?

Level key character 4: find the hidden message to discover a number.

When it is said thut an alternative treatment like homeospathy is useless, many people argue: 'But I have teken a homeopathic treatment, and it worked for me.' The reason such anecdotal evidence can't be used to see if sonething really does work is twofold. One is that the euidence is often indirect. It's oftem not 'I have taken' but 'I know someone who took'. There is a good reason why hearsay evibence is not accepted in court. It is all too easy for information to get corrupted when it is an indirect acceunt.

The other problem with arecdotal evidence is the placebo effect. If we compare the effect of, say, a homeopathic treatment and a sugar pill and know which is which, it is all too easy to say that the treasment is working and the sugar pill isn't. One reason for this is bicause we fool ourselves. If you asx ordinary wine drinkers which is better, wine from an expensive-looking bottle and wine from a cheap-looking bottle, they will say the expensive-looking wine tastes better, even if the two wines are identical.

But there is also a real side to the placebo effect. If we take something, for instance, that we think is an effective painkiller, our bodies release natural painkillers and opiate-like chemicals that reduce pain and help us feel better in ourselves. So just because a treatment makes the user feel better doesn't mean the treatment is actually doing anything.

SCIENCE FOR LIFE • BLIND TRIALS • 263

5. Researcher and research

Leakey – hominid

Goodall – chimpanzee

Fossey – gorilla

Galdikas – ?

Level key character 5: letter number of the fifth character of the solution.

6. Classification complete

Life–Domain–Kingdom–Phylum–Order–Family–Genus–Species

But one level of the hierarchy of biological classification is missing. What is it and where does it go?

Level key character 6: if life is level 1, domain is level 2 etc., what level is the missing classification?

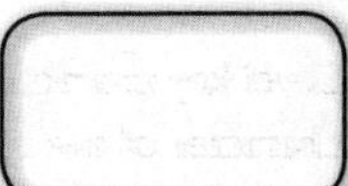

7. Morse menagerie

A message from an agent seems to be a list of some of the exhibits at the zoo.

> Platypus, bat, rhinoceros,
> Ant,
> Porcupine, ape, aardvark, elephant,
> Mole, bear,
> Cat, dog, seal,
> Pangolin, giraffe, bushbaby, armadillo, pig

We know she also had a Morse code chart (see opposite). Unfortunately, our cryptologists haven't managed to find the actual message. Can you?

Level key character 7: in the message.

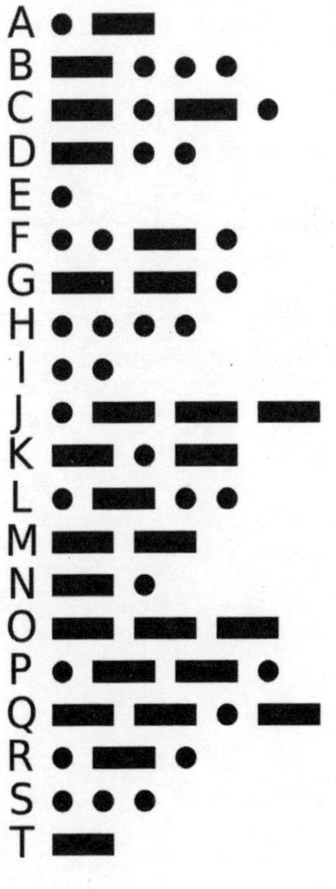
A
B
C
D
E
F
G
H
I
J
K
L
M
N
O
P
Q
R
S
T

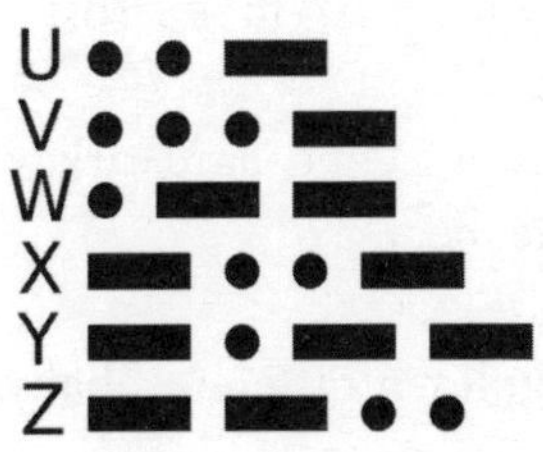
U
V
W
X
Y
Z

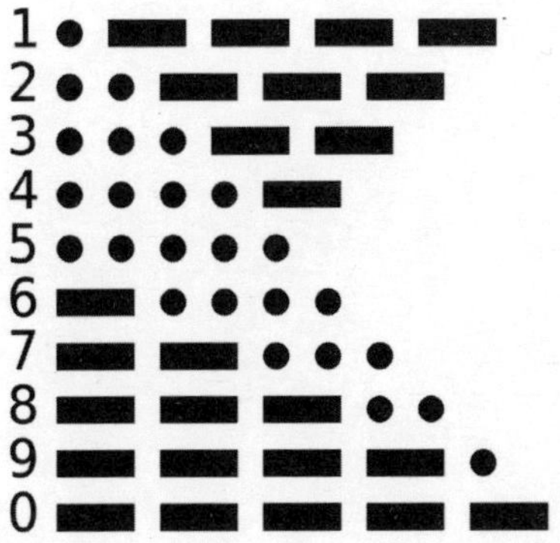
1
2
3
4
5
6
7
8
9
0

8. Collective birds

A field is packed full of swallows, peacocks, ravens and guineafowl. Get the right nouns initially to discover a number.

Level key character 8: the number

9. Organic oddities

Organic compounds (chemical structures of the types found in living things, though some are artificial) and genes sometimes have very silly names. Out of this list, how many are fake?

Arsole
Cheap Date
Crapinon
Frostysnowmene
Ken and Barbie
Luciferase
Lunatic Fringe
Penguinone
Pubescine
Rednose (derived from Rudolphomycin)
Sandwicensin
Sexithiophene
SNOG
Sonic Hedgehog
Spamol
Spock

Level key character 9: the number of fake names.

10. Protein chain

A biologist has sent this message, but the wording is a little suspect:

```
FOR OUR PURPOSES PROTEINS ARE ONE OR MORE

LONG CHAIN ACIDS, UNDER AN OVER-ARCHING

FORMAT. RESIDUES ARE BONDED TOGETHER.
```

Could there be a message hidden here? It's not a cipher – the key thing to remember about proteins is that you have to fold them correctly.

Level key character 10: read a number off an end of the manipulated message.

BIOLOGY - End of Level Guardian

You should now have ten numbers from the ten puzzles. Slot them into this table:

1	2	3	4	5	6	7	8	9	10

As a check, take number 1, multiply by number 2, divide by number 3, multiply by number 4, multiply by number 5, multiply by number 6, divide by number 7, divide by number 8, divide by number 9 and multiply by number 10: you should get 210.

Add up the ten numbers to get the Level 6 key.

Level 6 Key Number

It would be frustrating to get all the way through *Conundrum* and have one of your key numbers wrong, as you will need them all to crack puzzles in the final level. Here are two checks:

1. Add together the fourth, fifth and sixth level keys. Add together the digits of the answer. If the result has more than one digit, add those digits together – repeat until you have a single digit. The answer should be 1. (E.g. if the sum of the level keys was 529, adding together the digits gives 5+2+9 = 16. This has more than one digit, so 1+6 = 7, which would be the answer.)

2. Add together the individual digits of level keys four, five and six. You should get 28.

LEVEL 7 - TOYS AND GAMES

1. Colour conundrum

$$\text{red} + \text{brown} = 5$$
$$\text{blue} \times \text{green} = 15$$
$$(\text{black} - \text{pink} + \text{green}) \times \text{yellow} = ?$$

Level key word 5: choose the word with the number that is the solution:

1. WALL
2. WILL
3. WHO
4. WIN
5. WILT
6. WINE
7. WET
8. WIT
9. WON
10. WORN

2. Tricky tables

The game of backgammon is extremely old, with earlier versions often known as tables.

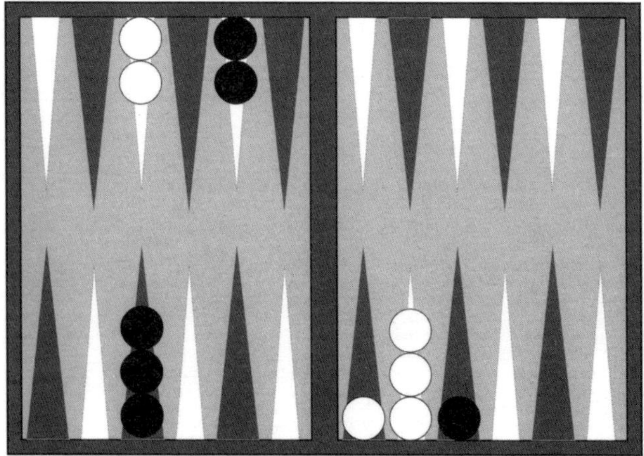

A board with this apparently part-played game was spotted through a spy's window. It's thought that it is being used to convey a message – but what? All we know is that this spy often uses ciphers that exclude X and Z and he has a preference for playing black. In backgammon, black and white alternate in play.

Level key word 9: crack the message and you will know which word to use.

3. Letters to numbers

O = 31.75
OO = 16.5
HO = 16.5
N = ?

Level key word 1: choose the word with the number that is the solution:

63.5 – DIP
63 – PIT
32 – LIP
31.75 – TIN
17 – BIN
16.5 – GET
16 – TAR
9 – POT
8.25 – FAR

4. Strange navigation

1. P-K4 P-K4
2. N-KB3 N-QB3
3. B-B4 B-B4
4. P-QN4 BxNP

Where is the black KB?

Level key word 6: choose the word with the number that is the location of the black KB.

KB3 – PAN
KB4 – WIT
QN5 – WET
QN3 – PEN
QB4 – TIP
QB5 – TOP
QN4 – TAP
QR4 – LOT
QR5 – LET

5. Mystery mail

The NSA has intercepted this email from a suspected traitor (underlining in original):

> Dear Professor,
>
> I think we will have to give our meeting a miss. You mustn't be too reverend about this, you know. Like all nuts, the kernel is the best bit. Be sure to play the English game and not the American.
>
> OAPE DHZOAWX CZ HNY
>
> … as they say in Minsk.
>
> Yours,
> Andrei

The untranslated phrase is clearly not Russian (or Belarusian). The NSA are sure it's a cipher, with the underlined words as the key – but using those specific words produces garbage. So what could the key be?

Level key word 4: given in the deciphered phrase.

6. Spelling numbers

If DOG = 5, FASHION = 13, AZURE = 14, FAX = 13 and QUICK = 20, which of the following list = 10?

LOG
FOG
COY
MOP
VAN
JOT
EAR
ZOO

Level key word 8: the word.

7. Checker draughts

The same spy who used to have a backgammon board on display, now has a draughts (checkers) board in sight of his window. He clearly isn't playing a game as the pieces aren't all on the same coloured squares. So, what is he up to?

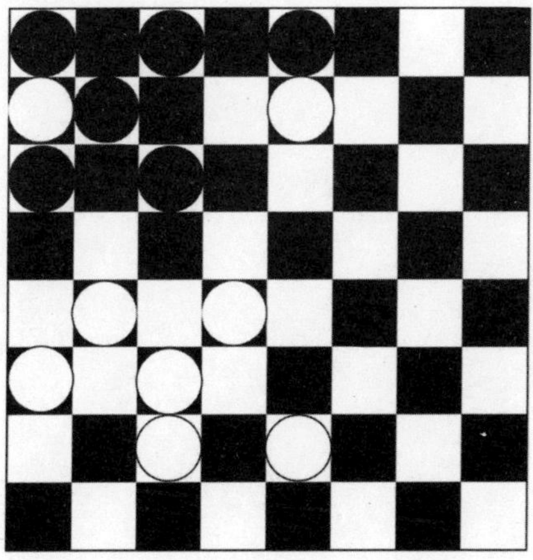

Also visible is a card with 'Black, white? They're all the same to me' on.

Level key word 7: is given by the position of the pieces.

8. Bridging the gap

This strange document apparently gives a clue to a number between 1 and 10. But what is it?

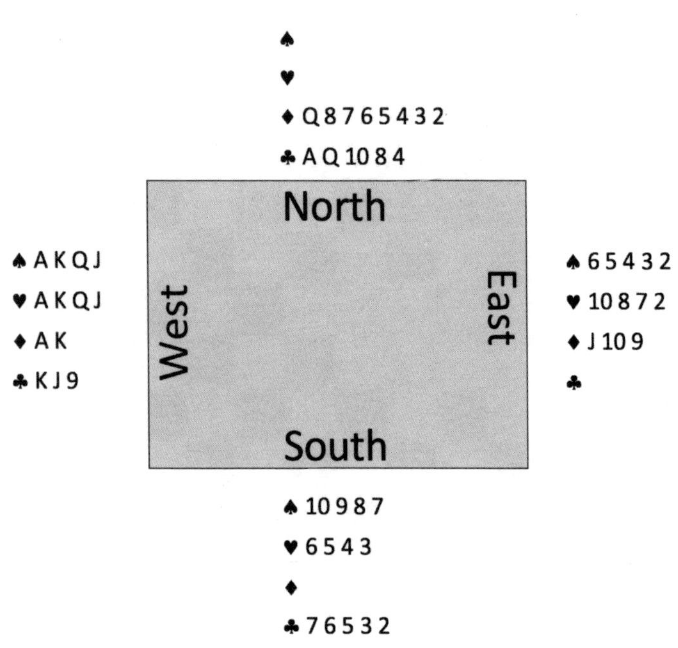

Level key word 10: choose the word corresponding to the number.

1 – PAT
2 – TAT
3 – MAT
4 – HAT
5 – RAT
6 – GAT
7 – BAT
8 – FAT
9 – CAT
10 – LAT

9. Address antics

If you turned from Boardwalk into Mayfair and from Indiana Avenue into Fleet Street, where would you turn from Atlantic Avenue, Oriental Avenue and Illinois Avenue?

Level key word 3: using the locations you turn into, take the first letter of the first location, the first letter of the final word of the second location and the first letter of the third location.

10. Matryoshka mathematics

These Russian Matryoshka dolls have been found in an old Soviet computing centre:

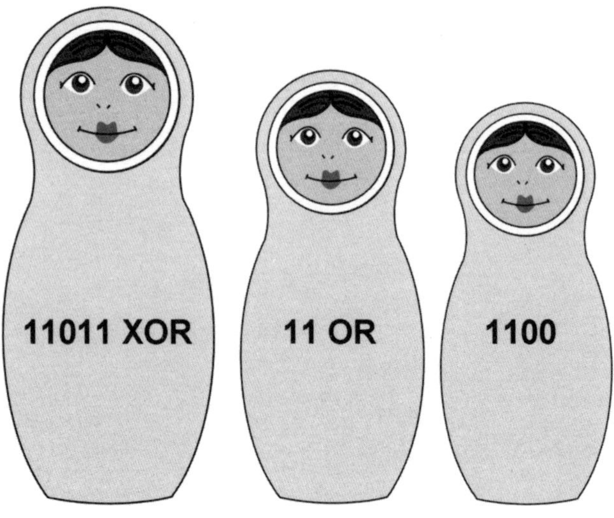

There's a message here ... but what is it?

Level key word 2: deduce the word from the writing on the dolls.

TOYS and GAMES - End of Level Guardian

Enter the ten key words here:

1. ____________________
2. ____________________
3. ____________________
4. ____________________
5. ____________________
6. ____________________
7. ____________________
8. ____________________
9. ____________________
10. ____________________

As a check, this should form a word ladder where each word has just one letter different from the previous one. For the level key number, add the number values of the initial letter of each word. (Remember, if you're using the online spreadsheet, you can use it to do this addition – see page 15.)

Level 7 Key Number

LEVEL 8 - ASTRONOMY

1. Binary astronomy

A group of astronomers decided to have some fun in the way they communicate with each other. It's not a secret cipher – they published exactly how they produce their odd coding – yet it has left many who have tried to decipher it scratching their heads. Here is the astronomers' explanation, plus an example enciphered letter to decipher.

> Each letter in the message is represented by its position number in binary. So A = 1, B = 10, C = 11 and so on. That binary value is then converted into a set of chemical symbols, where a metal represents 0 and a non-metal represents 1. So, to decode a letter, first substitute 1s and 0s for the elements, then convert that binary number into a letter.
>
> Here is a test letter: HePbHOS.

Level key character 3: the deciphered test letter.

2. Astronomical sequences

What types of body do these sequences describe?

1. MVEMJSUN
2. … IEGC …
3. OBAFGKM

Level key character 5: add together the number values (i.e. A = 1, B = 2, etc.) of the first letter of each of the three answers and divide by four to get the number value of the level key character.

3. Standard candles

Astronomers use a system called standard candles to measure the distance to a celestial body that is too far away to use parallax on. If we know two stars are the same brightness, but one appears dimmer than the other, the dimmer star is further away.

Although astronomers usually use 'magnitude' as the measure of a star's brightness, this is a logarithmic scale, which can be quite confusing. So here, to keep the maths simple, when talking about brightness we will deal with luminosity: energy output per second.

A star we know to be 10 light years away has a luminosity of 4 (in a scale based on the Sun at that distance being 1). A new star, which has the same luminosity, appears to only have a luminosity of 1.108. How many light years to the new star?

Level key character 9: the number value of this letter is the distance to the new star (round down if necessary).

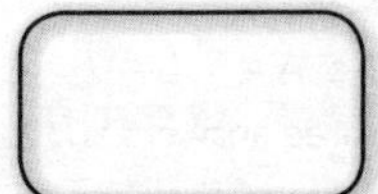

4. Punched particulars

A book on gravitational waves has been discovered in the library of a spy. One page has holes punched in it. It's clearly a message, but what does it say?

142 GRAVITATIONAL WAVES

when there was, at the time, no direct evidence of the existence of gravita█ional waves.

Unlike a ground-based observatory such as LIGO, LISA would have the c█ance to take in the whole of the sky. Rather than orbit the █arth as most satellites do, LISA is planned to be in an orbit around the Sun, following in the Earth's path at a distance of between 50 and 65 million █ilometres, about a quarter again the distanc█ at which the Moon orbits. The hope is that LISA would operate for a minimum of four █ears, but it has been designed to be able to stretch this to ten years if all goes well. █ISA's far longer int█rferometer 'arms' would enable it to deal with much lower-frequency gravitational waves than LIGO can de█ec█, in the rang█ between 0.001 and 0.1 Hz (█ipples per second).

This would enable L██A to detect waves from much higher-mass black holes, to explore th█ir role in galaxy formation and to use the interaction of t█ese huge black hol█s with other bodies to find out more about the black holes' event ho█izons and to t█st out black hole theoretical physics. It would also be able to predict coming mergers of smaller black holes up to a week before they occurred,

Level key character 7: mentioned in the message.

5. Astronavigation

If Heroditus is next to Aristarchus, you could climb Mons Rümker, and Russell and Eddington are neighbours, which mare or oceanum are you in?

Insularum (A)
Cognitum (L)
Serenitas (X)
Tranquillitatis (B)
Nectaris (D)
Nubium (M)
Humorum (S)
Vaporum (T)
Crisium (G)
Procellarum (E)

Level key character 2: the letter corresponding to the correct answer.

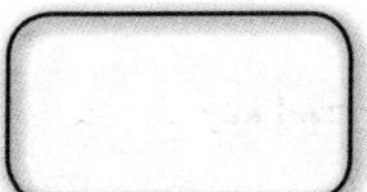

6. Constant confusion

Constants of nature, such as the gravitational constant, are essential for astronomical calculations. This simple code uses a constant of nature as its key. Many constants have never been precisely measured, so would be dangerous to use this way, but the ciphering astronomer has used a constant that can never change.

To get from the plaintext to the encrypted version, shift each letter forward by the appropriate number from the constant. Ignore any decimal points. If the constant isn't long enough, go back to the start. Decrypting simply reverses this process. So, for example, if the constant is 123 and the message is HELLO it is encrypted as follows:

Plaintext:	HELLO
Add:	12312
Encryption:	IGOMQ

The cipher text is:

DRBSNXIQSGH

Level key character 1: letter specified in the deciphered text.

7. Celestial cipher

An astronomically minded spy is using a simple substitution array cipher. To read off the plain text it's just a matter of matching the pair of key letters from the leftmost column and topmost row that match the letter in the body of the table. Unfortunately, we don't know what those letters are. Our only clue is the remark 'Nearest neighbour, cut short.'

KEY ⇓ ⇒					
	A	B	C	D	E
	F	G	H	I	J
	K	L	M	N	O
	P	Q	R	S	T
	U	V	W	X	Y

We do know that this cipher:
OCPNP NXN

Deciphers as:
MEET

Can you fill in the missing parts of the key and decrypt this message?
ICRCP MXNPN OEPCR EXMRC PNXCX EPMXE XMOE

Level key character 10: the letter that answers the question in the enciphered message.

8. Starry, starry night

I'm in Beta Persei but not in Alpha Tauri or Alpha Carinae. What letter am I?

Level key character 6: deduce from above.

9. Edmond's enigma

These numbers are a selection from a series (there are some gaps): 1066, 1145, 1456, 1682 and 1986. What number should immediately follow 1682?

Level key character 8: add together the digits in the answer to get the letter number of the character.

10. The name game

A sneaky astronomer has encrypted a message using an unknown key. The only hint is that he told a colleague to 'Think Cassegrainian and Gregorian'. This phrase isn't the key. But what is?

YWGHNWUCWVHFXBTYTI

Level key character 4: the penultimate letter in the decrypted phrase.

ASTRONOMY - End of Level Guardian

You should now have ten characters from the ten puzzles. Slot them into this table:

1	2	3	4	5	6	7	8	9	10

If you've got all ten correct, the guardian word should be astronomically significant. If it isn't, you've got at least one of the puzzles wrong – check them.

To work out the Level 8 Key Number add together the numeric values of all ten letters. (Remember, if you're using the online spreadsheet, you can use it to do this addition – see page 15.)

Level 8 Key Number

LEVEL 9 - MURDER MYSTERY

1. Introduction

This is a unique level. Instead of individual puzzles, the whole level is a single puzzle – a murder mystery you have to solve. Lindon Wells was a very rich man. A multi-billionaire, he lived as a virtual recluse in the penthouse which occupied the whole top floor of a building he owned in the centre of the city.

Wells was a very suspicious man. He was convinced that a number of groups were intent on abducting him for ransom or worse. Among those he suspected were the Mafia and a gang of international terrorists. He had also received threats from militant animal rights supporters, horrified at the way animals were treated in the laboratories of his company.

His food is provided daily on a cart, which is passed into the apartment through an airlock. One morning, the food cart arrived as usual. The caterer tried to put it into the air-lock, only to find that the previous day's cart was still fully loaded. After no response could be gained from Mr Wells on phone, text or electronic mail, his security manager decided to cut his way in. Wells was nowhere in the penthouse, yet it remained sealed, all doors and windows locked and bolted from the inside.

It is up to you to find out ... what happened to Lindon Wells.

You will discover information that will help you. This is made up of statements, physical evidence from examining the building, and other clues. You must bear in mind that anyone could lie in a statement, and this does not necessarily make them a kidnapper or murderer. The information you find will lead to a range of possible ways that Wells could have been made to disappear. It is up to you to deduce which is the most likely.

2. Suspects

Among the people legitimately associated with Wells were:

- William Bragg, chauffeur
- Louise Brooks, roof gardener
- Fred Earnshaw, chief accountant
- Phylis Latimer, personal secretary
- Simon Rankin, head of security
- Nigel Stoker, building receptionist
- Ryan Villa, caterer

... to whom you need to add the various groups possibly responsible for his demise.

3. Clues

1. A survey of the floor and ceiling of the penthouse proved conclusively that they had not been penetrated.
2. Miss Latimer's office was directly under Mr Wells' own office.
3. Mr Wells' favourite food was chicken liver paté. He made his own, using practically raw livers. He was also a heavy cigar smoker.
4. To find the size of the air-conditioning ducts, take the width (second number) of the kitchen from the width of the dining room and divide by 20.
5. A hot air balloon passed unusually close to the building during the early morning, nearly brushing against the kitchen window.
6. Surveillance cameras show that no other aircraft came within ten metres of the building.
7. There is nothing underneath the bath or behind the bath panels.
8. As standard procedure, the food trolley is searched by the security company, the receptionist and the caterer. It has a set of welded partitions on the inside which make it impossible for anyone to hide in it.
9. There was a period when the security camera in the lift was out of action, and it is possible that one or more people could have climbed on top of the lift itself unobserved.

10. Careful examination of the wall between the lift shaft and bedroom 1 proves that there was no access made that way.
11. The kitchen disposal shaft is only eight centimetres across. It has a grinder at the top, is regularly flushed with steam and has several sets of rotating knives down its length.
12. The kitchen disposal shaft was not used between Mr Wells' last phone call and the discovery of his absence.
13. Bedrooms and bathroom face north, kitchen and reception rooms face south.
14. A full search revealed no safe or cash in the building.

4. Scene of Crime evidence

A. Floorplan of the penthouse

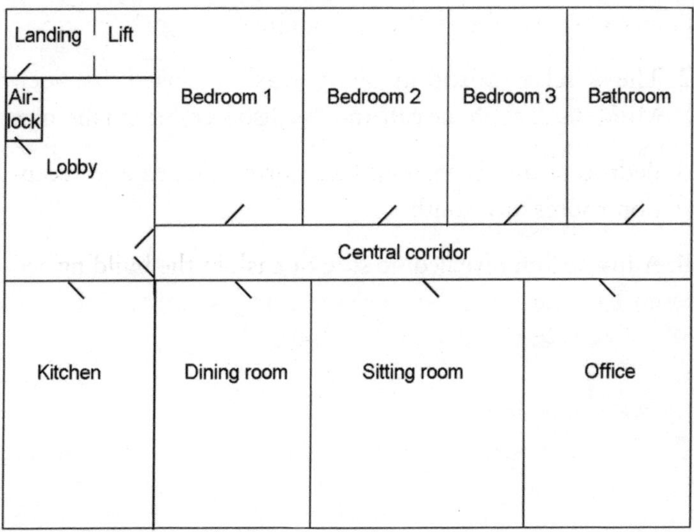

B. Room measurements in metres

Lobby: 9.4 × 6.0
Central Corridor: 3.6 × 21.4
Bedroom 1: 8.4 × 5.5
Bedroom 2: 8.4 × 5
Bedroom 3: 8.4 × 4.5
Bathroom: 8.4 × 4.2
Kitchen: 9 × 6
Dining room: 9 × 6.2
Sitting room: 9 × 8.6
Office: 9 × 6.6

C. Found in the kitchen

A large food processor with a blood-like, deep red fluid splattered inside it. A similar substance was found in the sink around the drain. It is currently being analysed. Windows sealed shut.

D. Found in the roof garden

The soil had been disturbed in a flower bed right over Mr Wells' bedroom.

E. Found in bedroom 1

There were fragments of a smashed piece of wood in bedroom 1, in the corner between the corridor wall and the wall of bedroom 2. Windows sealed shut.

F. Found in bedroom 3

The bedclothes of the bed in bedroom 3 were crumpled. Windows sealed shut.

G. Found in the sitting room

The principal feature of the sitting room was a large tank of piranhas. They would not eat for several days after the penthouse was discovered to be empty. A TV was on in the corner and there was a considerable amount of ash on the floor. Windows sealed shut.

H. Found in the office

A yellow sticky note attached to the personal computer screen in the office read 'Get that door catch fixed' in Wells' handwriting. Windows sealed shut.

I. Found in the dining room

There were strange scratches in the air-conditioning vent leading into the dining room, and the access hatch was not screwed in place. Windows sealed shut.

J. Found in the bathroom

The bath is extremely large and raised. It has a panelled side. Windows sealed shut.

K. Found in the airlock

The food trolleys are large, stainless steel trolleys which fill the airlock. They are more than big enough to hide a person (or a body) in.

L. Found above the lift

There is sufficient space above the lift, when at the top of the shaft, for several people to stand on its roof.

5. Background checks

A thorough check of balloon companies that could have provided the hot air balloon seen near the building revealed only one possible appropriate purchase:

Bigger
Balloon Boys

Hire of hot air balloon (standard model)	*£1,500.00*
Pilot's time	*£400.00*
Unsociable Hours	*£400.00*
Total	***£2,300.00***

Received with thanks from the Anivive Group (cash)

6. Witness statements

William Bragg, chauffeur

I only saw the old man once a year when he attended the Lord Mayor's Banquet, but he seemed to think it was necessary to keep on a chauffeur, just in case. I was in our office the night he disappeared, playing cards until about six in the morning. I didn't see anyone I didn't recognise go into the building through the back entrance, though I must admit I was distracted.

Louise Brooks, roof gardener

He has a beautiful garden on the roof, though I've never seen him in it. Perhaps he goes up at night; sometimes I've found things moved in the morning. If he does go up to the roof, he either comes out of his flat or has a secret entrance. The only access I know about is from the landing by his lift. I hear his flat is a strange place; he had three bedrooms, but never had anyone to stay.

Fred Earnshaw, chief accountant

The company is in excellent financial order; there's certainly no reason Mr Wells should abscond for financial reasons. Of course, he does keep all his reserves in cash somewhere in the penthouse. He never trusted banks – thought they wanted to rip him off. The company's reserves are in there too. But my confidence in Mr Wells is absolute. I think. He never told me where the money was, or anyone else, though he did say he was going to do an inventory of the reserves the day he disappeared. I just hope we can find it soon. Very soon.

Phylis Latimer, personal secretary

We had the strangest working relationship; I mean, there was no danger of him chasing me round the desk – we were never in the same room. I never met him in the flesh, never. I handled all his mail, converted it to electronic mail for him. He only ever spoke to me through the computer or by phone. Recently he'd had some very unpleasant threatening letters, from some of those so-called animal rights people. I mean, really disgusting, with, like, eyeballs and things in them. Gruesome.

Simon Rankin, head of security

I was aware, of course, of the threats from various terrorist groups, plus the rumours about Mr Wells' cash were well known among the criminal fraternity, but frankly this place was better protected than Fort Knox. All floors and walls are steel reinforced, the doors were like safes and the windows triple-glazed with bulletproof glass. I'd swear no one could have got in. There were the cameras too, of course – video cameras all along the access route, and they didn't pick up a thing. One broke down for a little while the night before, it's true, but that was only in the lift for half an hour or so, and I can prove that the lift never moved during that time. Explanation? Spontaneous combustion? I'm beaten by it, I'm afraid.

Nigel Stoker, building night receptionist

I was on duty the night before they found Mr Wells missing. I was already there before Miss Latimer left for the night – she used to work from an office on the floor below – and she'd spoken to him just before she left. I was still at my post when the caterer came in the morning and he found the other trolley untouched. There'd been some engineers looking at the problem with the lift camera during the afternoon; since that no one else entered – and this is the only way up to the old man's flat.

Ryan Villa, caterer

I took up the food cart as usual. There were three of us who did this job – we'd been personally vetted by the security guy. My wife thought that was hilarious – she always said I ought to be vetted. Normally it was no sweat, just swap the full trolley for an empty one that was left in this sort of airlock thing. It was specially made; just took the trolley: no room for anything else. Only that day, the trolley was untouched. Full.

7. Solution

So what happened to Lindon Wells?

1. He was ground up in the waste disposal by an intruder who hid on top of the lift.
2. He committed suicide by feeding himself to the piranhas.
3. He spontaneously combusted in the sitting room while watching TV.
4. He was trapped in a concealed safe between bedrooms 1 and 3 and was asphyxiated.
5. Animal rights protestors kidnapped him using a balloon.
6. The gardener abseiled down the side of the building and took Wells out the same way.
7. Miss Latimer made a hole through her ceiling and got in that way to taser and abduct Wells.
8. The Mafia arranged for a special food trolley with a sealed cavity which carried an assassin in and the body out.
9. A group of international terrorists got in through the air conditioning vents and abducted him.

MURDER MYSTERY – End of Level Guardian

Level 9 Key Number is the number of the correct solution.

Level 9 Key Number

LEVEL 10 - POLITICS

1. Scytale surprise

Ancient Greek politicians and military are said to have made use of an encryption device called a scytale. This was a multi-sided rod, around which a strip of leather or parchment was wrapped multiple times. The message was then written along the length of the rod, one face at a time. When the strip was unwrapped, the result was a string of letters which didn't make any sense until it was wrapped around the scytale again. Here's a piece of code from a sctyale strip:

THOUHIELWASTETNTIMTEISE.RYET

What was the original message?

Level key character 2: given in the deciphered text.

2. Political teatime

Which cake might you associate with the title of the person coming last after Victoria, Edward, Alice, Alfred, Helena, Louise, Arthur and Leopold?

Level key character 1: the letter that alphabetically precedes the third letter in the answer.

3. E pluribus unum

A history professor has a tendency to use the names of US presidents as the keys to her ciphers, selecting the presidential number corresponding to the day of the month. She sent this message on 3 August: discover what she sent.

NPTPITBFIZJJBHI

Level key character 8: the message will tell you which character to use.

4. Political sums

Divide the US President by the UK Prime Minister squared. Take away the UK Chancellor.

Level key character 4: convert the answer to a letter.

5. Meaningful Prime Ministers

Can you identify these British prime ministers (surnames only) from the meanings in their names? So, for example 'Christian place of worship/rise in ground' would be Churchill (church/hill).

1. Room/past participle of lie
2. Document describing bequest/male child
3. Person who constructs reed roofs
4. Fifth month/mandible
5. Mildly rejoicing/rock
6. Subterranean water-sources/shelter

Level key characters 9 and 10: to get character 9, add letter 1 of solution 5 to letter 3 of solution 2 and subtract the sum from letter 1 of solution 3. To get character 10 add together letter 6 of solution 1, letter 2 of solution 4 and letter 3 of solution 6.

6. Name numerics

If Tyler + Polk = 21 and Buchanan + Hayes = 34, what is Monroe + Taylor?

Level key character 7: convert the answer to a letter.

7. Euro blues

Though it's sometimes hard to believe what the Latin motto of the European Union means, all we need to crack this one is a single letter from that motto. Take the number of stars on the EU flag, divide by the number of procedural languages of the European Commission (as of 2019) and take away one. This tells you which letter from the motto to use (don't count spaces).

Level key character 3: the letter from the motto identified above.

8. African Union rules

The biggest political body in Africa is the African Union. Untangle these African Union countries based on a rule.

Here's a fairly simple one to show how the rules work. The rule here is the second word of the capital of Ethiopia. (Dashes simply indicate the absence of letters.)

CSEANTORTALOAMFREIACANNDREPPRUBILNICC-I--P-E

A bit more of a challenge. The rule here is the capital of Burkina Faso – but ignore O and U.

DBJMUIRBAUONULDTIII

Level key character 5: the fifth letter of the country that is G in the pattern.

9. Order, order!

If McMahon comes before Whitlam and Rudd before Gillard, what comes before Hawke?

Level key character 6: the fourth letter of the solution

10. Queen Mary's undoing

Ciphers have been used in political circles for hundreds of years. When Mary Queen of Scots was plotting the overthrow of her sister, Queen Elizabeth of England, she made use of a cipher that was mostly a simple substitution cipher, but with a few extras in the form of special characters that modified the message or contributed a whole word. Here is the alphabet A to Z (there is no J, V or W):

And here is a message using the cipher:

Level key characters 11 and 12: final two characters of the message.

POLITICS – End of Level Guardian

You should now have twelve characters from the ten puzzles. Slot them into this table:

1	2	3	4	5	6	7	8	9	10	11	12

If you've got all ten correct, the guardian phrase should be an instruction to calculate a number. If it isn't, you've got at least one of the puzzles wrong – check them.

To work out the Level 10 Key Number follow the instruction.

Level 10 Key Number

It would be frustrating to get all the way through *Conundrum* and have one of your key numbers wrong, as you will need them all to crack puzzles in the final level. Here are two checks:

1. Add together the seventh, eighth, ninth and tenth level keys. Add together the digits of the answer. If the result has more than one digit, add those digits together – repeat until you have a single digit. The answer should be 3. (E.g. if the sum of the level keys was 529, adding together the digits gives 5 + 2 + 9 = 16. This has more than one digit, so 1 + 6 = 7, which would be the answer.)

2. Add together the individual digits of all four level keys (Level 7 to Level 10). You should get 30.

LEVEL 11 - FOOD AND DRINK

1. Water into wine

I have two bottles, one containing water and the other containing wine. I pour one measure of wine into the water bottle. I then pour an equal measure from the water bottle back into the wine bottle. Both bottles are analysed and it turns out that there is just as much water in the wine as there is wine in the water.

Which of the following have to be true to make this possible (you can choose more than one):

1. The bottles are the same size.
2. The water and wine are thoroughly mixed after the measure is poured into the water bottle.
4. The wine and water have to be thoroughly mixed after the measure is poured back into the wine bottle.
8. The wine has the same density as the water.
16. The water and wine are miscible.
32. None of the others have to be true.
64. It is impossible to be certain that there is just as much water in the wine as there is wine in the water.

Level key number 6: add together the numbers of all the statements above that have to be true.

2. Drinks order

I've been given an order of beer, gin, sherry and wine as the key to a cipher. Unfortunately, it doesn't work in the alphabetical order given. We need another clear ascending order of the same drinks to decipher the message.

ATZ FBNR SNUGWJ MPWS

Level key number 10: given in the deciphered message

3. Peachy keen

We're looking for a person who links a peach dessert and a type of toast.

Level key number 5: letter number of the fourth letter in the person's first name.

4. Recipe for success

Whip together a tub of whipping cream and 50 grams of caster sugar until the mixture forms soft peaks. Stir in 50 millilitres of wine and the zest and juice of half a lemon. Transfer to small bowls or glasses and decorate with lemon zest.

If the first is 27, the second is 20 and the third is 16, what is this question?

Level key number 2: answer to the question.

5. Mixology

Use five parts of the liqueur produced by Carthusian monks (green or yellow), seven parts of an orange liqueur produced in Saint-Barthélemy-d'Anjou and three parts of the berries that are used to make a Danish liqueur named after a Norwegian winter sports resort. Don't shake or stir. What have you got?

Level key number 1: the number that results.

6. Recipe for disaster

6 chicken breasts
3 tbsp red curry paste
3 tbsp olive oil
? tins coconut milk
2 lemongrass stalks
2 large onions
? tbsp plain flour
1 × 200g tin water chestnuts
1 piece of fresh ginger
1 × 250g pack green beans
1 lime
1 tbsp brown sugar

This recipe has got wet and two of the numbers have been obscured. We know the person who wrote it loves mathematical sequences and puzzles. What are the missing numbers likely to be?

Level key number 8: add together the two missing numbers.

7. Fruity conundrum

I'm using my blender when A SEPARABLE PAN SNAPS.

Which three fruits was I mixing up?

Level key number 9: add the number values of the first letter of each fruit.

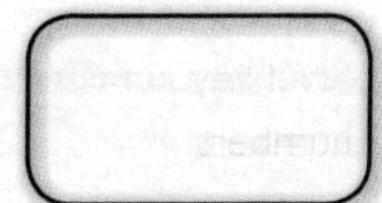

8. Food and drink words

If we ignore their meanings, which is the odd one out in this list of food and drink words?

FOOD, DRINK, JELLY, FIZZ, CHILLI, BACON, EGGS, EELS, FUGU, BEEF, LAMB, PORK.

Level key number 3: the number value of the first letter of the odd one out.

9. Tasty cipher

The password to get into a secret meeting is a foodstuff. It has been encrypted as

IZMBGI

The encrypted password was accompanied by the instruction 'Play fair with a testing typewriter sentence. I=J, you know.'

We also know that spy sending the password had some blank grids like this.

Level key number 7: add up the number values of each letter in the foodstuff and divide by two.

10. Can you read RDA?

Nutrition information		
Typical values	*Per 100g*	*% of GDA*
Energy	61 kcal	3.8
Protein	4.9g	13.6
Carbohydrates of which sugars	6.9g 6.9g	3.7 9.6
Fat of which saturates	1.5g 0.9g	2.7 5.5
Fibre	0.01	0
Salt of which sodium	0.2 0	5.9 4.2
Calcium	198mg	26

We often ignore the nutrition information on the side of a pack. Here's some of the information for a yoghurt, which is being used to convey a sequence of digits for a code. The first nine digits are 9, 5, 7, 3, 6, 1, 1, 7, 6 – what is the tenth digit?

Level key number 4: the answer.

FOOD AND DRINK – End of Level Guardian

You should now have ten key numbers – fill them in below:

1	2	3	4	5	6	7	8	9	10

If you've got all ten correct, starting with the first, the next is bigger, smaller, bigger, bigger, bigger, smaller, smaller, bigger, smaller. Five are even and five are odd. Only three of them are prime numbers.

To work out the Level 11 Key Number add together all the numbers:

Level 11 Key Number

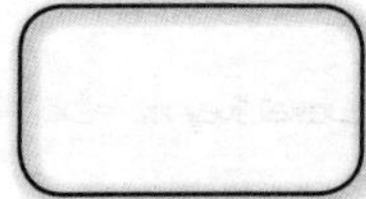

LEVEL 12 - MATHEMATICS

1. Irrational rhymes

Can I hide a hairy crocodile,
Or slowly tarry the while?
Findings suggested waiting impatient 'til an end.

This a pretty horrible poem, but it forms part of a large collection of very specialist literature. What is the creation of this specific kind of literature called?

Level key word 7: the word for the creation of this type of literature

2. Barbershop logic

A barber shaves every man in town who does not shave himself, and only those men who do not shave themselves. Does the barber shave himself?

Think about it.

This is an approximation to a mathematical paradox about a set of all sets that are not members of themselves, known as Y's paradox, where X Y is a person's name.

Level key word 9: Run XY together and take the seventh, tenth, fourteenth and fifteenth letters.

3. Complex conundrum

If I=J, A=–2+2i, E=2+2i and Z=2–2i, what does –2+2i, –1–i, –1, 1, 2–i, –1–i spell?

This grid might be useful:

			0		
0					

Level key word 5: the answer to the puzzle above.

4. Sequential story

If
B–1+17–4 = BARN

and
M–12+19–12+11 = MATHS

what is
I+5–10+5–2+8?

Level key word 2: the solution

5. Red pill or blue pill

A mathematician working on a new secret communication device has died without revealing to anyone what his computer password is. It's thought that this cryptic inscription hides the password. But what is it?

$$\begin{pmatrix} C & A & B \\ D & A & A \\ B & D & E \end{pmatrix} \begin{pmatrix} C \\ A \\ B \end{pmatrix} = \begin{pmatrix} ? \\ ? \\ ? \end{pmatrix}$$

Level key word 4: the solution.

6. Infinite possibilities

A mathematician suspected of espionage has encrypted this short message with a straight key. The only clue we have is the words 'Dangerous to encounter. But as small as infinity gets.' It's thought that the first sentence refers to the plain text and the second to the key.

Here is the encrypted message:

QUWQVVV

Level key word 6: the solution.

7. Problem children

I have two children. One is a boy born on a Tuesday. What is the probability I have two boys?

Choose an option from the list below. Taking the first option as an example, '1 in 4' means out of four possible outcomes, one is that I have two boys; while '1 in 2' is the same as 50:50 or 50 per cent.

1 in 4 – SAUCE
7 in 24 – DRESSING
8 in 27 – BARBECUE
1 in 3 – MAYONNAISE
10 in 27 – SALT
9 in 24 – FRENCH
10 in 24 – MUSTARD
12 in 27 – CAESAR
11 in 24 – PIRI PIRI
13 in 27 – KETCHUP
1 in 2 – VINEGAR

Level key word 1: the word corresponding to the correct answer.

8. Word addition

ABOVE+

BEGIN+

CHIN+

POV+

AH+

J

_____

?????

Level key word 10: the solution.

9. Bayesian bugs

It's claimed that the new test for a common disease is 95 per cent accurate. When someone takes the test, 95 per cent of the times it is given, if it says you have the disease, you do have it. In 5 per cent of cases it will say you have the disease if you don't. It will never come up negative if you have the disease. The test is given to a million people a year, of whom 1 in 2,000 have the disease.

I take the test – and the result is positive. What's the chance I have the disease? (Round the answer if necessary.)

1 in 101 (0.99 per cent) – IOTA
1 in 100 (1 per cent) – ROTA
1 in 99 (1.01 per cent) – META
1 in 5 (20 per cent) – METE
9 in 40 (22.5 per cent) – MOTE
1 in 4 (25 per cent) – MITE
11 in 40 (27.5 per cent) – LITE
1 in 2 (50 per cent) – LATE
189 in 200 (94.5 per cent) – BATE
19 in 20 (95 per cent) – FATE
191 in 200 (95.5 per cent) – TATE

Level key word 8: the word for the appropriate chance.

10. Yorkshire cipher

The security services have discovered a cryptic message. The sender was a mathematician. It was accompanied by a single bit of Yorkshire dialect: 'Eeh, by gum!' Cryptographers have guessed the key, but the result is still a cipher. It seems the grid below does the final untangling, one way or another. But what's the key, and how to finish the process?

VZBPYAFWFXVTJDSXYU

Level key word 3: given when deciphered.

MATHEMATICS – End of Level Guardian

Enter the ten key words here:

1. ____________________
2. ____________________
3. ____________________
4. ____________________
5. ____________________
6. ____________________
7. ____________________
8. ____________________
9. ____________________
10. ____________________

As a check, the first letters of each word should spell KIDNAPPING and the final letters of each word should spell PORTRAYALS.

For the level key number, add together the number values of the second letter of each word. (Remember, if you're using the online spreadsheet, you can use it to do this addition – see page 15.)

Level 12 Key Number

LEVEL 13 - SPORT

1. Football results

A soccer fan site is in the habit of posting totally spurious results. The security services have begun to suspect it is something shady. Here's their latest set of results:

Swansea City 3–7 Leicester City
Everton 5–1 Arsenal
Ross County 5–7 Partick Thistle
Aston Villa 1–3 Watford
Tottenham Hotspur 1–1 West Bromwich Albion
Newcastle United 2–1 Leeds United
Liverpool 3–2 Derby County
Barnsley 2–1 Middlesbrough

Find the message enciphered in the scores.

Level key character 3: the time as a number.

2. Field sums

If

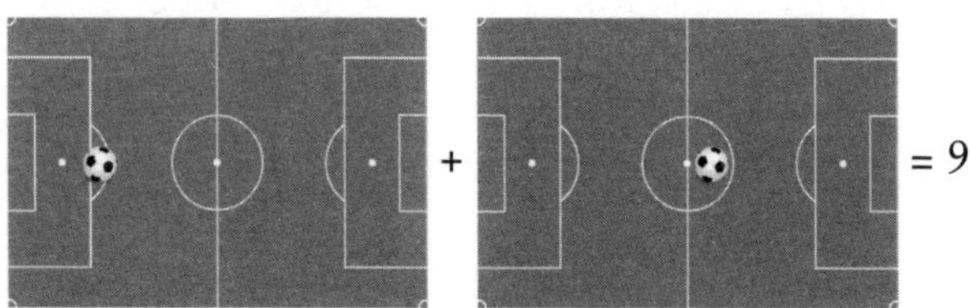

and

what is

Level key number 8: the answer.

3. Triangular diamond

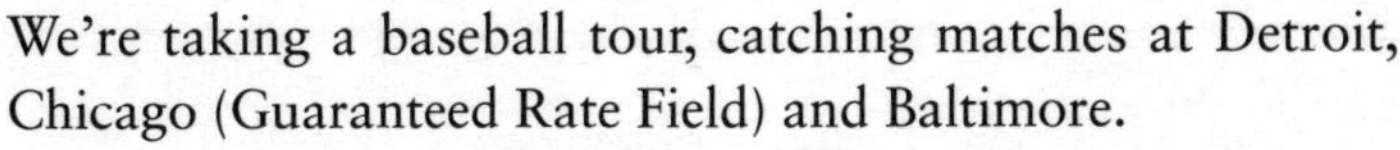

We're taking a baseball tour, catching matches at Detroit, Chicago (Guaranteed Rate Field) and Baltimore.

Level key character 9: deduce a number from the first letters of the key missing information.

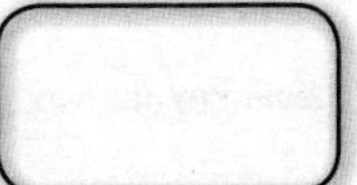

4. Scoreboard

A new game is being devised where a team can compete in 100 different trials, scoring from 1 to 100 if they win. So if a team won all 100 trials they would score a total of 1+2+3+4 … +100. What is the highest number the scoreboard would need to show for a team?

Level key character 1: the highest possible score.

5. Rugby tour

If we fly from the capital of the westernmost Six Nations country to the easternmost Six Nations country, which of these is closest to the great circle distance:

1475 miles
1425 miles
1375 miles
1325 miles
1275 miles
1225 miles
1175 miles
1125 miles
1075 miles
1025 miles

Level key character 4: the closest number of miles in the list above.

6. Find the soccer key

MI5 has discovered this grid, shown below, which they think is associated with the message intercepted from a spy, probably about a safe. Unfortunately, they don't have the key. The only possible clue is a text, sent by the spy to a confederate: 'I'm off to see Liverpool this week and Fulham the week after. Both starting as home games.'

Key 2 / Key 1						
	6	M	Y	8	D	I
	F	C	2	R	4	S
	0	G	L	J	Q	H
	W	7	T	3	Z	P
	B	K	X	U	A	5
	1	Ø	E	9	N	V

NRFCARECANLEEEIAANFCLEANNNIVENLV

Level key number 2: the number you need to open the safe.

7. Firsts

If Hines, Smith and Greene all did it for 100 in 10, who did it for 1 in 4?

Level key character 10: letter value (A=1, B=2, etc.) of the third letter of this person's surname.

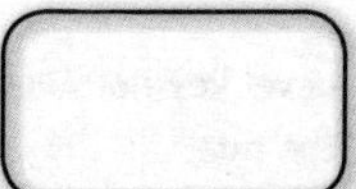

8. Olympic oddities

Some of the following have been events in the modern Olympic Games, with medals awarded during at least one Games between 1912 and 1948. But which?

- Architecture
- Applied arts and crafts
- Dramatic literature
- Drawings
- Epic literature
- Etchings
- Knitting
- Lyric literature
- Metalwork
- Music
- Paintings
- Sculpture
- Town planning

Level key character 7: the number of genuine disciplines in the list above.

9. Links

Which actual person links the Olympic 100 metres freestyle, Edgar Rice Burroughs and John Clayton?

Level key character 6: letter value (A=1, B=2, etc.) of the first letter of this person's surname.

10. Olympic village

The security services have retrieved this map of an Olympic Games site with handwritten annotations. The annotations were thought at first to be event dates, but this has been ruled out; instead, it is believed they carry a message. The list of letters along the bottom is clearly relevant too, but isn't a cipher. What is the message?

Level key character 5: the code number in the message.

Olympic Village

Central events

E
15, 5, 10

A
6, 14, 16

D
3, 10

B
4, 5, 9, 2

C
6, 7

G
10, 16, 25

F
4, 5

Key

A – Main stadium: athletics

B – Velodrome

C – Main pool

D – Rowing lake

E – Shooting and fencing

F – Diving

G – Gymnastics and weight lifting

AAA E BBBFGEDCCFDEGGB

SPORT – End of Level Guardian

You should now have ten key numbers – fill them in below:

1	2	3	4	5	6	7	8	9	10

If you've got all ten correct, from 1 you go down to 2, down to 3, up to 4, down to 5, down to 6, down to 7, down to 8, down to 9 and up to 10. The total of all 10 is 6,870.

To work out the Level 13 Key Number, add together the first digit of each number.

Level 13 Key Number

LEVEL 14 - TRANSPORT

1. Alphabetti spaghetti

If UM becomes NIFOR, QC becomes UEBE and HL becomes OTE, what becomes RAV OME OVEMBE?

Level key word 1: run together the three answers and drop the final letter.

2. Manhole mystery

We have intercepted a message from an operator who likes to use the markings on manhole covers in nearby roads as the keys to his ciphers. An agent has copied the letters on the latest cover used into his notebook: MH.

We have deciphered the encrypted message, but unfortunately this is what the plain text comes out as:

ODYPTHKPNHRDMSDHBDGS

MH was clearly the wrong key. It was definitely the right manhole cover, and the letters on it were definitely used as the key. So where did we go wrong? What does the message say?

Level key word 6: the password.

3. Licence to thrill

US car licence plates often carry a state nickname. If we pass cars with:

- The Natural State
- Ocean State
- Peach State
- Native America
- Live Free or Die

on their plates, which states have they come from? (Note: one state no longer regularly issues with this nickname, but it is still available.)

Level key word 9: made up from the initial letters of the five states, in the order of the list above.

4. Streetwise

There's a lane in the north-east corner of Higher Walton (UK), north of the River Darwen, that is reminiscent of a literary wizard. Find the postcode for this location.

Level key word 4: the chemical element with the last character of the postcode for the location above as its symbol.

5. Flying a message

In one of the most bizarre attempts recorded to pass on a secret message, a spy has taken an extended plane trip. Her journey took her from Yellowstone Regional Airport (Cody, Wyoming) to Terrance B. Lettsome International Airport (Tortola, British Virgin Islands) to Sila Airport (Papua New Guinea) and finally to General Heriberto Jara International Airport (Veracruz, Mexico).

Level key word 8: code word given in the message.

6. Road trip

People often think that E-numbers make children hyper-active. But if I drove from Amsterdam to Rome via Cologne, Frankfurt, Basel, Lugano, Milan and Parma, what E-number would keep me going all the way?

Level key word 2: the chemical element with an atomic number matching the number given in the answer.

7. Tube tangle

I'm at Notting Hill Gate. I take three stops north to my first destination the end of the District Line. I head off, changing at King's Cross St Pancras, proceeding via Angel and Elephant and Castle, continuing two more stops to my second destination. Finally, I retrace my route, changing at Bank to the westbound Central Line. My third destination is three stops after Shepherd's Bush. Quite a journey.

Level key word 7: the first letters of my starting point and the three destinations.

8. Stationary solution

We've found this hand-drawn map. It's apparently a European city. But what are the six locations that are marked?

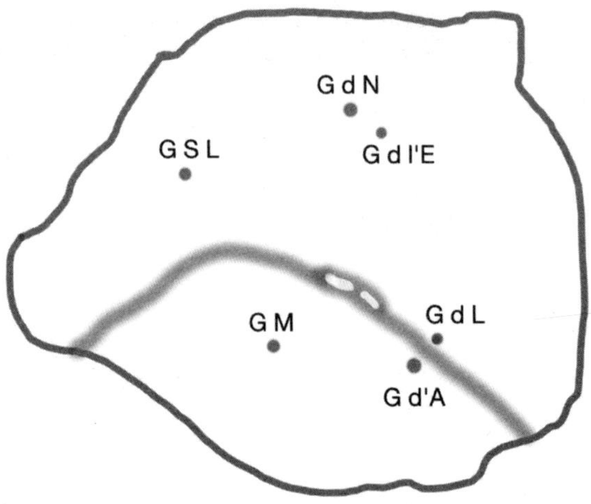

Level key word 3: the chemical element with the symbol that's the same as the last two letters as the location marked G M.

9. Flight of fancy

The security services have found this boarding pass, used as a bookmark by a spy:

The passenger name seems odd. Scribbled on the back of the boarding pass is 'Ignore times: elsewhere, digits are individual.' Can you decipher the message?

Level key word 10: the deciphered message.

10. Linear location

Visiting a World Heritage Site in Peru, you see a huge monkey with a spiral tail. Add up the number of fingers (including thumbs) and toes the monkey has.

Level key word 5: the chemical element with the atomic number of the sum of fingers and toes.

TRAVEL - End of Level Guardian

Enter the ten key words here:

1. ______________________________
2. ______________________________
3. ______________________________
4. ______________________________
5. ______________________________
6. ______________________________
7. ______________________________
8. ______________________________
9. ______________________________
10. ______________________________

All the keywords are chemical elements. As a check, the first letters of each word should spell out BBSNPGNSAR.

For the level key number, add together the atomic numbers of the ten elements and divide by two.

Level 14 Key Number

It would be frustrating to get all the way through *Conundrum* and have one of your key numbers wrong, as you will need them all to crack puzzles in the final level. Here are two checks:

1. Add together the eleventh to fourteenth level keys. Add together the digits of the answer. If the result has more than one digit, add those digits together – repeat until you have a single digit. The answer should be 3. (E.g. if the sum of the level keys was 529, adding together the digits gives 5+2+9 = 16. This has more than one digit, so 1+6 = 7, which would be the answer.)

2. Add together the individual digits of all four level keys (Level 11 to Level 14). You should get 39.

LEVEL 15 - TV

1. Seaside surprise

I am not in Portmeirion. Okay, but what number are you?

Level key character 9: the number.

2. Grid show

We have this cipher grid from a spy who is also a fan of award-winning TV shows. The two key words used to produce letter pairs from the inner grid are missing – but if we can work out the show, they are usually surnames of central characters. The only problem with this approach is that the keys may contain duplicate characters. If so we have try all possible options and see which works.

Key 2 / Key 1						
	S	T	E	R	L	I
	N	G	C	O	P	A
	B	D	F	H	J	K
	M	Q	U	V	W	X
	Y	Z	[SPACE]	[COMMA]	[STOP]	[DASH]

Here's the message, enciphered using the grid:

SROANDNAORODNALDORLDOANE

Level key character 3: the number specified as the key.

3. Follow my leader

If an actor playing the Doctor has the same surname as a fictional doctor who says he isn't – among other things – a bricklayer, which number do we need for the Doctor?

Level key character 2: the number.

4. Strange thing

This grid was found in Hawkins, Indiana in the 1980s. It should decipher the message below with keys WEIRD and WORLD, but it doesn't work. The fault seems to be with Key 1. Decipher the message.

Key 2 / Key 1					
	A	B	C	D	E
	F	G	H	I/J	K
	L	M	N	O	P
	Q	R	S	T	U
	V	W	X	Y	Z

DLILIRELRWILEORODDELDDIWDDWWDDIR

Level key character 8: in the message.

5. Unlikely links

What institution links actor Hugh Laurie (TV shows include *House*), writer Robert Harris (TV shows include *Have I Got News for You?*), actor Tom Hollander (TV shows include *The Night Manager*) and the author of this book (TV shows include *Christmas University Challenge*)?

Level key character 1: the number value of the first letter of the answer to this question.

6. The name game

If (Sarah ≈ Alison ≈ Helena ≈ Cosima ≈ Rachel) ≡ Tatiana what TV show are we watching?

Level key character 6: the number value of the first letter of the answer to this question.

7. A curse on both

If Urquhart turns into Underwood, what happens to Elizabeth?

Level key character 7: the number value of the second letter of what Elizabeth becomes.

8. Downton delight

First names of three Crawley daughters in age order (oldest to youngest), followed by their mother's first name, supported by the surnames of Charles, Elsie and Thomas. Add upstairs to downstairs, taking away 26 if necessary to keep below 27, to get the key. To make things trickier, the first nine characters of the key are in the top table and the second nine characters in the second table.

Upstairs									
Downstairs									
Key									

Upstairs									
Downstairs									
Key									

Now decipher this:

JJOSVTVNHDSMPFAPCC

Level key character 4: the Abbey's score.

9. Del Floria's Finest

If Ilya was 2 what was Napoleon?

Level key character 10: Napoleon's number.

10. Simpsons strategy

Homer Simpson has a habit of repeating an unsuccessful action over and over again in the hope it will eventually succeed. He has thought up an enciphering technique and applied it to his own name to get:

HWBRWKBVCIHC

He has also applied the same technique to another *Simpsons* character. Identify:

SBMIXAWLYQQ

Level key character 5: number value of the last letter of the character's name.

TV - End of Level Guardian

You should now have ten key numbers – fill them in below:

1	2	3	4	5	6	7	8	9	10

If you've got all ten correct, the pattern from 1 to 2, 2 to 3, etc. is down, up, down, down, up, down, down, down up. Five have single digits, five have double digits. And there are six answers that are prime numbers.

To work out the Level 15 Key Number, start with the first number you've written in the table above, add the second, take away the third, add the fourth, and so on to the tenth.

Level 15 Key Number

LEVEL 16 - TECHNOLOGY

1. Computer glitch

I have written a computer program to write out all the numbers between 1 and 1,000 as words. (To make the output shorter, the program writes 'and' as '&' – e.g. 'two hundred & thirty-one'.) One of the functions of the program is to add up the number of times each letter crops up in the whole list. But it surely has got the number of 'A's wrong.

How many letter 'A's are there in my table of all the numbers between 1 and 1,000 as words?

Level key number 5: the number.

2. Dodgy data

The security services have intercepted a book sent to a spy. One of the pages contains markings that are clearly intended to convey a cipher text and a key.

128 BIG DATA

on personal history. All these systems can do is try to find some link between the two. But remember the mantra that correlation is not causality. Even if you can find measures that seem to match with future job effectiveness (and usually that linkage isn't available – the selection of predictive data is just at the whim of the system designer), the chances are this is just coincidental correlation, not causality.

There are websites that are set up to discover spurious correlations in data (see chapter 8). There, we discover that US crude oil imports from Norway correlate with drivers killed in collisions with railway trains, that the per capita consumption of mozzarella cheese is correlated with the number of civil engineering doctorates awarded, and that

Decipher the message.

Level key number 1: given in the message.

3. Artificial insolence

Our Artificial Intelligence bot, Eliza, is hiding a code number. But you will have to get it out of her. The good news is that we know the exact words required to get it: 'Code please' (without the inverted commas). The bad news is that Eliza can be evasive. You might have to ask more than once.

Visit Eliza at www.universeinsideyou.com/experiment10.html and have a chat.

Level key number 9: the code number.

4. Does not compute

((27 AND 31) OR (NOT 25)) XOR 6 = ?

Warning, the numbers above *and the solution* are in octal (base 8). You'll need to convert the numbers to binary before applying the logical operations specified.

Level key number 3: the solution.

5. Morse mixup

–··– –·–– – –· ––– – ––· ––– –

––– –– ·––·

There is no cipher – it's plain text ... but something's not right.

Level key number 6: given in the message.

6. Computing giants

We've found this cipher array, but don't have the keys. All we know is that they involve big names in computing and that any duplicate letters in the keywords are omitted (i.e. only first use of the letter is included).

Keys								
	C	B	E	I/J	O	Y	K	R
	S	Q	T	D	H	A	W	M
	P	L	F	N	U/V	Z	X	G

Decipher this:

```
BCIOBRBSIS MCIRMCBCIS IRBMBCBOIC MOBSMIMOIC
```

Level key number 10: in the message.

7. I'll ask ye once and once only

This simply enciphered message has been intercepted by GCHQ, who are experts on standard codes for information interchange.

77 101 101 116 32 97 116 32 53 112 109 32

84 114 97 102 97 108 103 97 114 32 83 113

117 97 114 101

What does it say?

Level key number 7: the number in the solution.

8. Console wars

The key to decrypt this message is the name of Commodore's mightiest computer range followed by the Japanese name for the SNES (Anglicised spelling).

XUJAJLOXWWKUVVHHFJK

What does it say?

Level key number 2: the number in the solution.

9. Super clean

It was originally thought that a spy was smuggling out plans for a new cyclonic vacuum cleaner. But the message below was received from the same source.

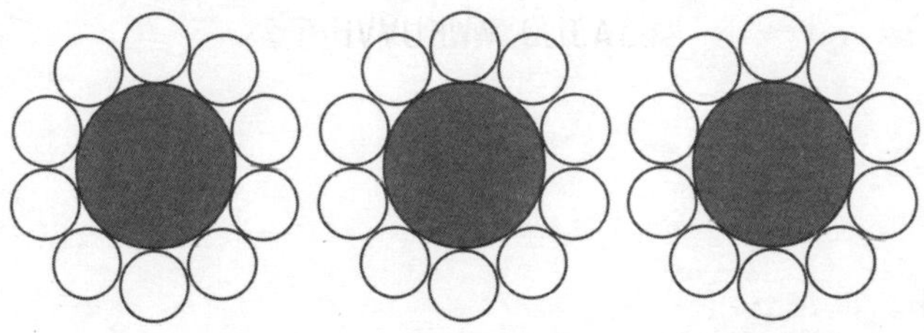

INCETVILAS TTUNSEIAUO IVCRENSEMA

What does it say?

Level key number 8: the number in the solution

10. Odd connections

What is the number of lines in the 1850 version of the original verse from which the words around Apple's first logo were extracted? (Note, this poem is often shown without verses, in which case how many lines from 'The Evangelist St John' to the end of the Apple extract, inclusive.)

Level key number 4: the number of lines

TECHNOLOGY - End of Level Guardian

You should now have ten key numbers – fill them in below:

1	2	3	4	5	6	7	8	9	10

If you've got all ten correct, from 1 to 2, 2 to 3, etc. you go up, up, down, down up, down, up, down, up. There are two prime numbers. Six have single digits, four have double digits. To work out the Level 16 Key Number, add together the first digit of each number smaller than 45.

Level 16 Key Number

LEVEL 17 - ART

1. Multiple meanings

Whose (attributed) painting could be named after a jewelled headband, or an ironmonger's wife or even a royal mistress?

Level key word 3: letters 14, 8, 6 and 4 of the artist's name (omitting any spaces).

2. Abstract encryption

This intriguing piece of abstract art opposite was submitted to a London gallery regularly visited by a known spy.

When the spy was later searched he was found to be carrying a piece of paper with this on it:

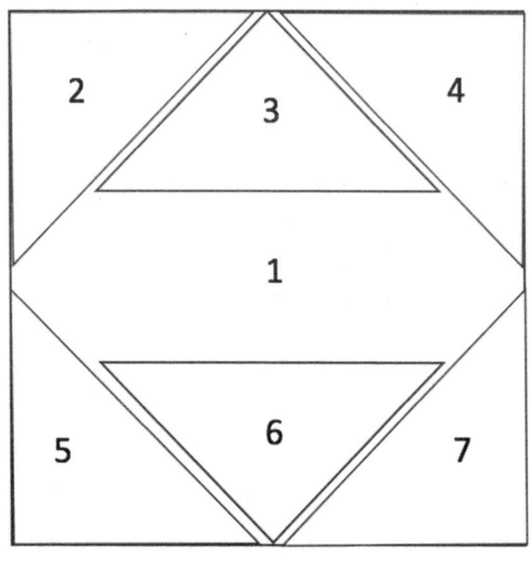

0 = A	1+3 = I...
1 = B...	2+3 = N...
7 = @	5+7 = SPACE
1+2 = H	6+7 = STOP

Level key word 8: in the message in the artwork.

3. Making a good impression

Where did the painter of *Coquelicots, La Promenade* produce many works featuring his garden and pond?

Level key word 7: first four letters of the answer.

4. Cubist conundrum

This arty image appears to have letters embedded in it. But what does it say?

Level key word 9: the word you are instructed to employ.

5. Dürer's Melancholic square

Use a 1514 woodcut to identify the character numbers you need to spell out a four letter word.

	1	4	2
			3

Level key word 6: the word.

6. Beer goggles

What is the brand of beer shown in Manet's *A Bar at the Folies-Bergère*?

Level key word 2: the answer.

7. But is it art?

This Pop Art image is titled *Fence Defence.*

Apparently, it's a clue to help decipher this message:

TRNSHDEEEYEAWODROUIL

Level key word 5: in the deciphered message.

8. Rotary art

A photograph of this work of art, displayed in a gallery window, was found on an agent's phone.

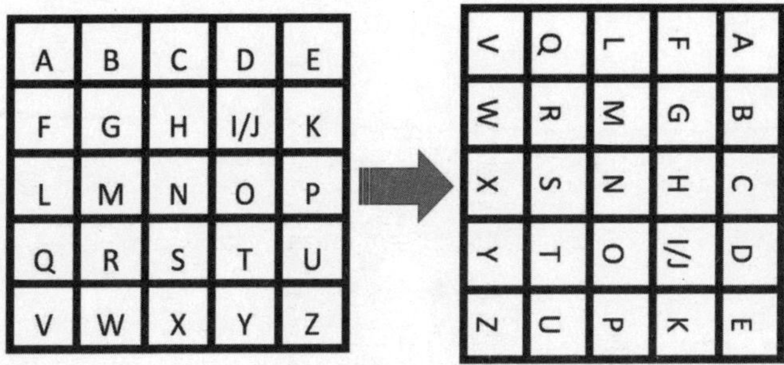

It seems to be linked to this message:

SVBADOAHWIMABAKUHTFZGZV

Level key word 10: in the message.

9. Palaeolithic designs

According to its notes, this artwork provides an interface between the symmetry obsession of modern physics and the artisanship of the nail technician.

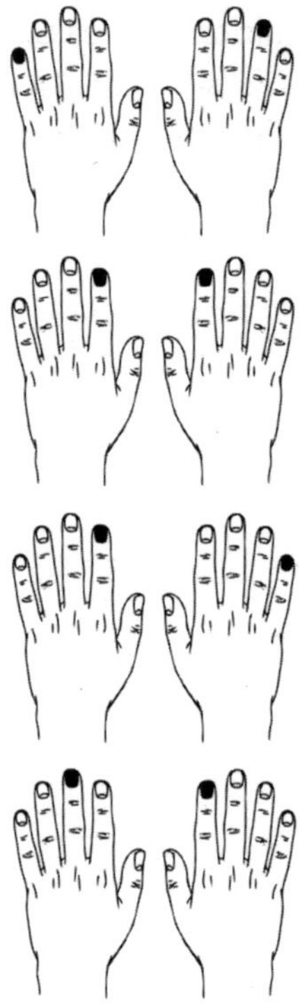

But suspicion has been roused by the artist's signature on the back of the work, which looks like I=J. Could it conceal a message?

Level key word 4: in the message.

10. Arty surnames

An exhibition features 20th-century artworks: *Shadow Play* (1990), *American Gothic* (1930), *The Persistence of Memory* (1931) and *Guernica* (1937), in that order.

A spy visited the exhibition and passed on his catalogue to someone else. The words 'surnames' and 'run together' were underlined and the following numbers were written on the catalogue: 11, 6, 17, 5.

Level key word 1: deduce from the information above.

ART – End of Level Guardian

Enter the ten key words here:

1. ____________________
2. ____________________
3. ____________________
4. ____________________
5. ____________________
6. ____________________
7. ____________________
8. ____________________
9. ____________________
10. ____________________

As a check, each should be a four-letter word. The initial letter of each subsequent word should be higher in the alphabet than the previous one. The final letter of each subsequent word should be lower in the alphabet than the previous one.

For the level key number, add the number values of each final letter. (Remember, if you're using the online spreadsheet, you can use it to do this addition – see page 15.)

Level 17 Key Number

It would be frustrating to get all the way through *Conundrum* and have one of your key numbers wrong, as you will need them all to crack puzzles in the final level. Here are two checks:

1. Add together the fifteenth to seventeenth level keys. Add together the digits of the answer. If the result has more than one digit, add those digits together – repeat until you have a single digit. The answer should be 4. (E.g. if the sum of the level keys was 529, adding together the digits gives 5+2+9 = 16. This has more than one digit, so 1+6 =7, which would be the answer.)

2. Add together the individual digits of all three level keys (Level 15 to Level 17). You should get 22.

LEVEL 18 - PHYSICS

1. Einstein's finest

$nd^2wm^2cs^2zp^2br^2pf^2tj^2mc^2br^2br^2mc^2$

$zp^2wm^2nd^2iy^2tj^2xn^2pf^2iy^2jz^2mc^2br^2$

Level key character 3: letter indicated in the message.

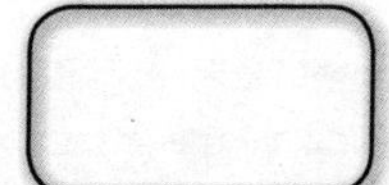

2. Pointers

A book was found in a spy's library with this page folded over.

THE QUANTUM AGE

phosphor. Glass itself is mildly phosphorescent when hit by a stream of electrons, hence the original ghostly green glow that Crookes and the other experimenters saw, but a phosphor gives off a much brighter light. In a phosphor, the incoming electrons smash into the atoms in the lattice of the material. Some of their kinetic energy is absorbed by the electrons orbiting the atoms of the phosphor, boosting them from the fixed valence band to the higher-level conductance band, where they can drift through the lattice until they reach specially introduced impurities called activators. Captured by the activator, the electron drops down in level and gives off energy in the form of a tiny flash of light – a scintillation.

In the back of the book was written: Add the number values of the indicated letters (there are five of them), subtract 1 and divide by 2.

Level key character 6: follow the instructions to deduce the letter.

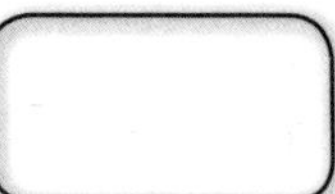

3. Quark code

This intercepted email is either pure nonsense or contains a hidden piece of information:

```
SUPER CAPON NEEDS LATER TROT TENOR
```

It doesn't appear to be a conventional cipher – it's suspected that there is some sequence of selecting letters (counting spaces) that will produce the hidden message. But what is it?

Level key character 2: the letter whose position in the alphabet is described by the hidden message.

4. Names and dates

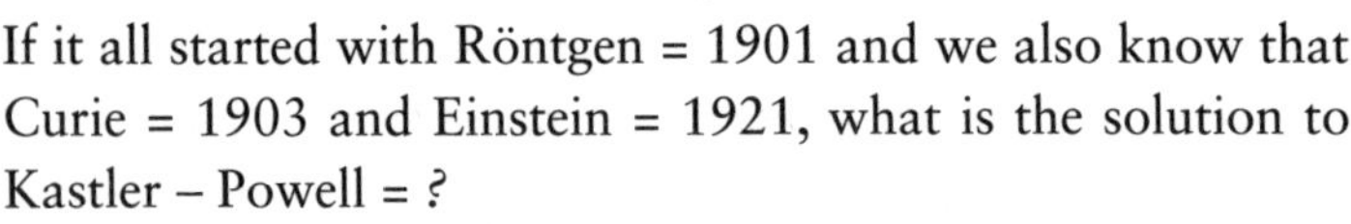

If it all started with Röntgen = 1901 and we also know that Curie = 1903 and Einstein = 1921, what is the solution to Kastler – Powell = ?

Level key character 10: the letter with the number value calculated above.

5. Anagrid

The security services have been lucky enough to get hold of this array, containing an encrypted message.

A	E	F	M	N	N	Y
D	E	W	E	T	E	N
S	M	O	E	U	K	A
T	E	R	A	O	H	T
N	R	U	E	T	G	A
O	U	S	C	D	E	S
–	B	E	K	K	O	O

Remember the topic of this level.

Level key character 7: the codebook letter.

6. Particulars

We have intercepted a message from a physicist who usually employs a key cipher. This text seems to be a hint for finding the key phrase: 'Six fundamental names (avoid truth and beauty). Increasing mass ☺'

VBTWXPXNDFHAJUVVEOGGMYKRH

Level key character 4: the letter with the position in the alphabet identified in the message.

7. Gravity of the situation

The same dubious physicist is at work again. We think this email is intended to pass on a single number. But what is it?

> Let us assign arbitrary units such that:
>
> $$G = 4$$
> $$m_1 = 8$$
> $$m_2 = 11$$
> $$r = 4$$
>
> Then the Newton's force will succeed.

Level key character 9: the letter with the number value that is the result.

8. What's in a name?

Born in Nice in 1731, this physicist measured the density of the Earth using gravity. One of the world's most famous physics laboratories was given his surname (or could it be the name of a Duke of Devonshire?) What is that name?

Level key character 1: the second letter of the answer.

9. Starry mystery

Take the chemical symbol for the heaviest element that can be made in a normal star without it going supernova or colliding. Add together the number values of the two letters in that symbol for the answer.

Level key character 5: the answer is the number value of this letter.

10. Symmetry rules

Symmetries are very important in modern physics. All the conservation laws (energy, momentum etc.) have a corresponding requirement for symmetry if the situation is shifted in time or space, or reflected or rotated, etc.

We have intercepted what appears to be Morse code using only paired numbers, corresponding to the number values of letters.

To make it more challenging, numbers up to 99 have been used; these can be deciphered by repeatedly taking off 26.

We've given the Morse code for the digits in the table opposite. Unfortunately, the message below, already deciphered from Morse to pairs of digits, is garbled. Bearing in mind the sender works with symmetry in his day job, and would find it natural to apply a change of symmetry to the Morse codes before transmitting them, what could be wrong with our deciphering? What does the message really say?

Transmitted message

63, 91, 27, 10, 5, 64, 38, 53, 92, 81

With extra 26s removed

11, 13, 1, 10, 5, 12, 12, 1, 14, 3

Deciphers as

KMAJELLSNC

Level key character 8: given in the message.

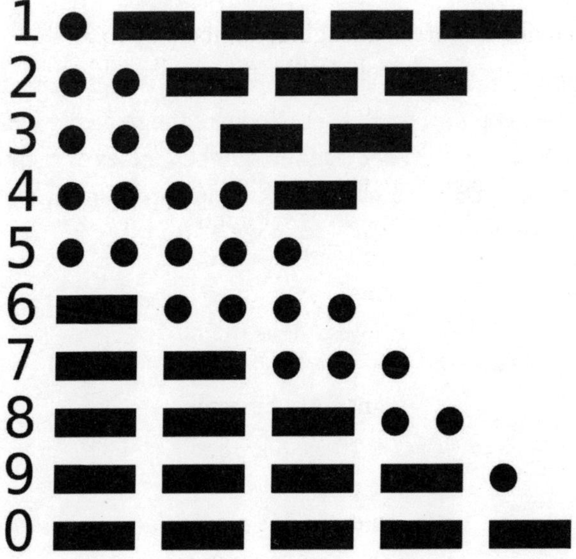
1
2
3
4
5
6
7
8
9
0

PHYSICS - End of Level Guardian

Enter the ten key characters here:

1	2	3	4	5	6	7	8	9	10

As a check, the letters should form two distinct sequences – there is a jump part way through where the sequence changes. For the level key number, add the number values of each letter. (Remember, if you're using the online spreadsheet, you can use it to do this addition – see page 15.)

Level 18 Key Number

LEVEL 19 - HISTORY

1. Date data

Follow the year of the Gunpowder Plot to blow up the English Parliament with the year of Henry III of England's second coronation. Turn this into a skinny four-letter word.

Level key word 10: the answer.

2. Roman mystery

A message from Julius.

OARNW MBAXV JWBLX DWCAH VNWUN WMVNH XDANJ

ABRLX VNCXK DAHLJ NBJAW XCCXY AJRBN QRV

Level key word 6: what UNWM deciphers as.

3. Elizabethan echoes

That time of year thou mayst in me behold
When yellow leaves, or none, or few, do hang
Upon those boughs which shake against the cold,
Bare ruined choirs, where ____ the sweet birds sang.

Mr Shakespeare at his historical best. What's missing?

Level key word 3: the missing word.

4. It's Greek to me

The ancient Greeks sometimes used lower case letters to represent numbers (they would have used a ' symbol on each to indicate it wasn't a letter, but they're omitted here for simplicity):

$$\iota\gamma,\ \varepsilon,\ \iota\delta,\ \delta$$

Level key word 7: the spelled-out word using number values as letters.

5. Oxford oddity

An Oxford historian had an apparently failsafe method of remembering his computer password. Here's an entry in his address book:

Dr Mirabilis sermo:littera.
Subtract two from each, then subtract relevant city.
12:7, 6:4, 15:1, 13:5.

The wording on the cover of the address book is transcribed below. Can you work out his password?

ROGERUS BACON
Philosophus insignis Doctor Mirabilis
Qui methodo experimentali
Scientiae fines mirifice protulit
Post vitam longam strenuam indefessam
Prope hunc locum
Inter Franciscanos suos
In Christo obdormivit
A. S. MCCXCII

Level key word 5: the spelled-out word.

6. The cipher of Bonacci's boy

Work out the key to decipher this message:

EPPRYPNOM

Level key word 2: according to the text, what shouldn't you do?

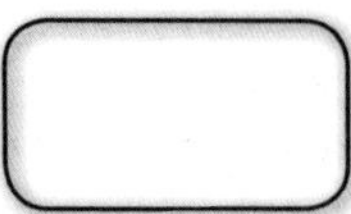

7. Equestrian enigma

Four historical horses which once had a great view, inside for their own protection ... but they're still outside too:

Where are we?

Amsterdam – PANE
Antwerp – SANE
Florence – FANE
Glasgow – CANE
London – DANE
Porto – VANE
Venice – LANE
Vienna – BANE
Warsaw – MANE
Weimar – WANE

Level key word 4: the four-letter word corresponding to the correct city.

8. Common ground

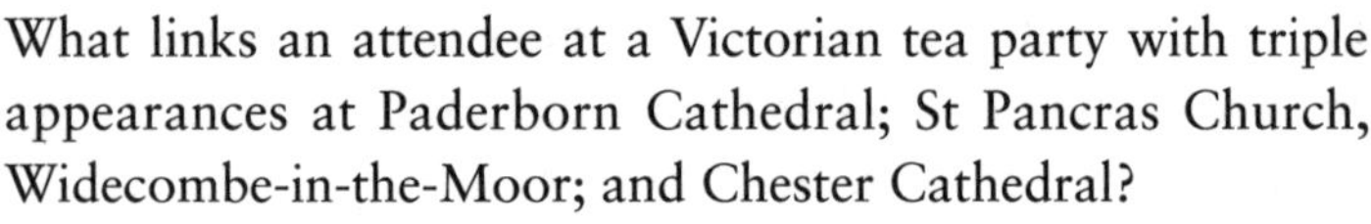

What links an attendee at a Victorian tea party with triple appearances at Paderborn Cathedral; St Pancras Church, Widecombe-in-the-Moor; and Chester Cathedral?

Level key word 1: the word linking all four things.

9. American arrangement

The security services have intercepted a letter from a spy operating in America. The return address on the letter was 20 Breckonridge Street, Gettysburg PA.

VAPLH QXMRE CILSP RSKYF SLJSN

Level key word 9: the only four-letter word in the plain text.

10. Prehistoric puzzle

The Stonehenge monument is one of the most famous in the world. At its height, it had 35 lintel stones, each linking two uprights. A Stonehenge expert is found dead. He has scrawled this sequence on a piece of paper:

1, –7, 0, –8

He also wrote '1 becomes current number of lintels+4. Transform each number similarly.' Which four-letter word do we spell out?

Level key word 8: the word spelled out.

HISTORY - End of Level Guardian

Enter the ten key words here:

1. ______________________________
2. ______________________________
3. ______________________________
4. ______________________________
5. ______________________________
6. ______________________________
7. ______________________________
8. ______________________________
9. ______________________________
10. ______________________________

As a check, this should form a word ladder where each word has just one letter different from the previous one. For the level key number, add the number values of all the initial letters. (Remember, if you're using the online spreadsheet, you can use it to do this addition – see page 15.)

Level 19 Key Number

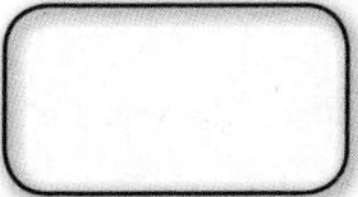

Key number catch up

As you will be using them in the final level, it might help to bring forward the nineteen level key numbers from earlier levels:

1	
2	
3	
4	
5	
6	
7	
8	
9	
10	
11	
12	
13	
14	
15	
16	
17	
18	
19	

LEVEL 20 - CRYPTOGRAPHY

1. Get cracking

XQLUOEKULUHJXEKWXJJXQJCYDTIQHUSYFXUHI

Level key value 1: antepenultimate word of the deciphered text.

2. No key required

An extract from a book (not a complete sentence). Consists of 100 characters, including spaces. For clarity, spaces have been replaced by dashes.

```
FE-IUF-S-WURILTOACTENINLH

R-IH-DN----SEITAGDRTTENNE

M-IEHHACKNETSSAERE-DNHCUT

-C-O-AEOL-THAFTL-VTWR-S-O
```

Level key value 2: number of words beginning in T in the solution.

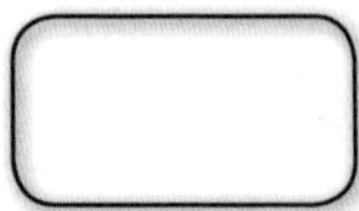

3. Bar none

The only clue we have to deciphering this cryptogram is 'Faith's Buffy catchphrase alphabetically – omit X.'

Level key value 3: the letter specified in the solution.

4. Guardian's key

The key to decrypting this message is revisiting your first level key numbers.

MCWBYJ

Level key value 4: the deciphered word.

5. Poetic promise

Decipher the poem (rhyme scheme ABACB) and then find a number in it. '=' indicates a space as part of the cipher text – ordinary spaces are just dividers, not part of the cipher text.

```
TAFWT HROHH EMRIE REMCR EDEHE ==D== HO=OI

ANINS PLNL= PY=YA I=M== NWYIS EI==P STDHE

SHEAC ==EVI IDPEA SE==L =LSF= BIPOP OGAUL

UHCNA NTEDC D,,,E .===,
```

Level key value 5: the number.

6. Flowery sequence

This plant name has been encrypted by using the level key numbers 7, 8 and 10. Note individual digits are being used for each letter in a systematic but not consistent way.

GCDDREIN

Level key value 6: the deciphered word.

7. Random rubbish?

For a while it was assumed that this secret message was corrupted as it doesn't make a lot of sense – and it's not a conventional cipher. But there is a message.

AMY SWEETS TREAT MATES BAD. PATER

PASSED OUTER WHALE, LITTLE DECIDED

ABOUT ORANGES RESISTING PEELS.

ROVER SPENT AND LAPPED LAMPS.

Level key value 7: the hour in question.

8. Digraph dilemma

We know that this enciphered text uses an array cipher with I=J and a horizontal and vertical keyword. The letters in the grid use the title of a Star Wars movie as key phrase. We don't know the keywords, though we do know the keywords are words and not random letters.

GTNBNERAGENBNERBGAGENENBGAGBAENENERAGARARAR

SLBRAAANEASGARAASLSRSLBNBGALENENBGAASNERARS

LBRBNBRSATGSNEREGAGENTLENEATGSNENEASRSNANTG

ENTGBGENTNANEGERSNAGAABNELSRSLBGSGTGALSGERS

GENBNERBGAGENE

Level key value 8: last word of the decrypted text.

9. Navigate by numbers

We're nearly there. Just one to go after this one. Solve it by the book. (We're all friends here: no titles required.)

7:1:8:2, 22:3:3:3, 28:1:2:7, 65:3:1:1, 274:3:10:2

Level key value 9: the word spelled out.

10. Enigma variation

This is a cut-down version of the Enigma machines used during the Second World War by the Germans and cracked at Bletchley Park. The operator presses a letter, the current flows through the wiring as indicated and lights up the letter it emerges at. Then the right-hand wheel rotates one position. The effect of this is that every connection on either side of the rightmost rectangle moves down one. If either end falls off the bottom, it now connects to the top instead. Then another letter is pressed, and so on. It's symmetrical – works for enciphering or deciphering. Decipher the following word from the starting position below:

HGL

Level key value 10: the deciphered word.

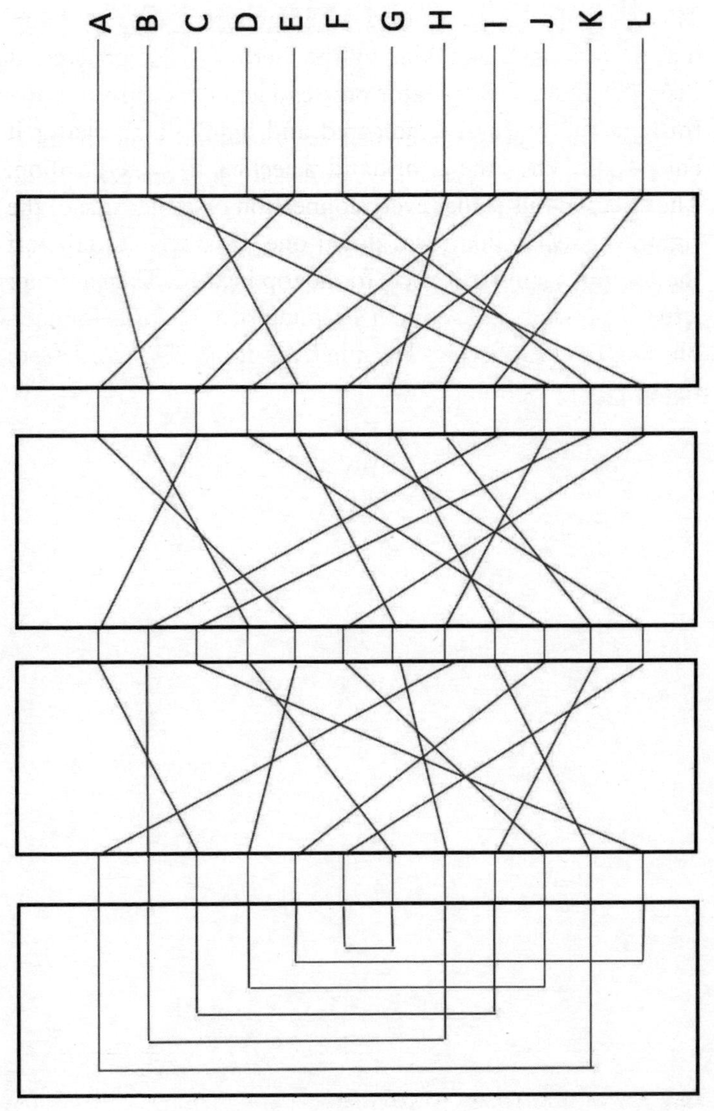
A
B
C
D
E
F
G
H
I
J
K
L

End of level Guardian - Final submission

You now have everything you need to submit your solution. Go to www.ConundrumBook.com and click on 'Enter solution' (scroll to the last page of the site if using a phone). The solution is each of the key values from this level (separated by spaces) followed by the sum of the key numbers of levels 11 to 19.

Good luck!

Hints

Level 1 – Literature

1.
This is the kind of cipher that the puzzle's name suggests. Note a three-letter word appears twice. What's likely to be the most common three-letter word? Use that to crack the cipher.

2.
Just do what it says. Find these book titles with numbers in them.

3.
To read the message you need to take a letter from the same position (e.g. the last letter of the book's title or the first letter of the publisher's name) from each book in turn. It should spell out a time.

4.
'... And What Alice Found There' is the end of the title of a famous book. The first part of that book's title tells you how to look at the plain text provided to find out the enciphered text.

5.
Acrostic.

6.

To find the key, take away the letters of PRIDE AND PREJUDICE from the letters of the cipher. As described in the Cracker's Guide, this means taking away the number of the alphabet (e.g. P = 16) from the number of that character in the cipher, then convert the resultant number back to a letter of the key. If the result is negative, add 26 to make it positive.

7.

Magwitch is from *Great Expectations*, Pecksniff from *Martin Chuzzlewit*, and Weller from *Pickwick Papers*. The other two you can work out.

8.

All you have to do is find the opening letters of this book and subtract them from the enciphered text (if you aren't sure how to do this, see the Cracker's Guide). You will need a specific edition of the book, identified by the clue about a king.

9.

The first author is a 'sounds like' for the author of the *Foundation* series and *I, Robot*. The second is an anagram of the author of *The Moon is a Harsh Mistress* and *Stranger in a Strange Land*. The final author is an anagram of an author best known for fantasy but who wrote *Fahrenheit 451*.

10.

You don't need to read Latin to guess which city the phrase *Nunc ubi Regulus aut ubi Romulus aut ubi Remus?* refers to. Look for obvious names. And the answer is just one letter different from the English in the Latin/Italian form.

Level 2 – Geography

1.
Think of a very small country in Europe. If you're struggling with the spelling, you may find that there's an extra character you didn't expect shortly after the L.

2.
These are the UK Shipping Forecast sea areas. The missing sea area is named after the most northerly point on Ireland.

3.
We're clearly looking for a word to bridge the gap between the two countries.

4.
While we don't know for certain, a good guess is that the letters in the left-hand column go down in alphabetic order. We can work out from the cipher which letters to include.

5.
When you dial the UK from abroad you start '44'.

6.
The countries are listed by looking across a map of Africa, heading East. When you fill in the missing countries you will get a sequence of initial letters. Replace those with their position in the alphabet (A=1, B=2 etc.) The result is a well-known numerical sequence. All you have to do is work out the next number in the sequence and provide that letter of the alphabet.

7.

In the UK some railway stations have identifying names after the place – e.g. Manchester Piccadilly or Bristol Temple Meads. The letter contains four of these identifying names. Pair the station name with its town or city.

8.

It's a simple substitution cipher. Find the country in the list beginning with the letter in the cipher (e.g. Z is Zambia). Replace it with the first letter of a word associated with that country, suggested by the message.

9.

Just follow the instructions. The two-letter code produced is not a state abbreviation.

10.

The key to decoding the message is the difference between time zones for these locations. Starting at Kuwait with the initial K, use the time zone difference (e.g. Kuwait → Uruguay, then Uruguay → Alaska, etc.) of each jump of location to work out the next letter. Make sure you avoid daylight saving times and use standard times.

Level 3 – Movies

1.

These are quotes from movies, but which movies?

2.

The choice was between two of the top ten grossing movies of 1977.

3.

In each case the missing word is a movie directed by the person on the left, which is also something or someone that features in the film on the right.

4.

There aren't many letters appearing frequently enough to be the repeated indicator letter – just try them and see if the result makes any sense.

5.

Do the math.

6.

It would help to know the book that *Blade Runner* is (very loosely) based on.

7.

There's a sequence of numbers that the plain text hints at. You will need to take these away from the letters of the cipher (i.e. shift back down the alphabet). Note that the sequence gets bigger than 26. See the Cracker's Guide on sequence shift (page xiii) for an easy way to deal with this.

8.

Come up with the movie titles suggested with a (missing) number in them and do the arithmetic on the numbers. For example, if we'd had 'angry men divided by men and a baby, that would be *Twelve Angry Men* and *Three Men and a Baby* so 12/3 = 4.

9.

The clue should reveal three character names from a movie.

10.

To encrypt the message, the spy wrote the plain text in the circles above the text. Then subtracted the value of the letter below to the left (if there was one) and added the value of the letter below to the right (if there was one). So in this example:

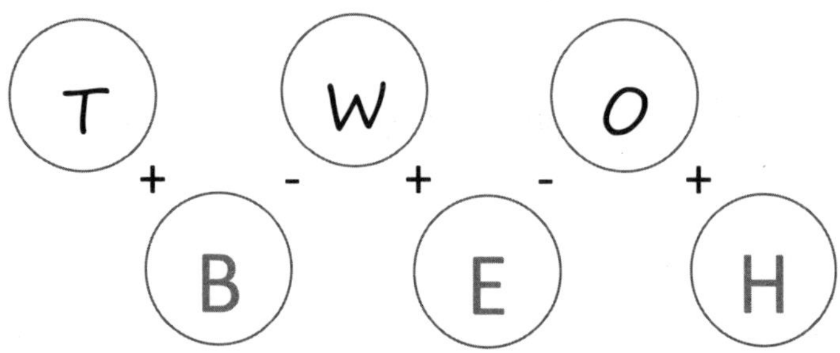

T would be encrypted by adding 2 (for B) producing V, W by subtracting 2 (for B) and adding 5 (for E) producing Z, O by subtracting 5 (for E) and adding the value for the next letter below, and so on.

To decrypt, the process would be reversed. So decrypt the first letter by subtracting 2 for B, decrypt the second letter by adding 2 for B and subtracting 5 for E, and so on.

Level 4 – Chemistry

1.

Match each compound to its source, then read off the letters.

2.

It has been encrypted by turning each letter in the plain text into the equivalent number (A=1, B=2, etc.), looking up that atomic number on the periodic table and finding the equivalent 'eka' atomic number.

3.

Find a way to slot the text into the diagrams, then read off the decrypted message around each ring.

4.

We need to go from atomic number to letter number.

5.

Match each substance to its date of discovery, then read off the letters.

6.

Ignore the chemical symbols – just read the message as a sequence of numbers.

7.

Find a letter from each part of the sentence, in that order.

8.

Note that one name, although better known as a fictional substance, is the name of a real molecule, and so counts as real.

9.

This list consists of two key letters from the name of each element, sorted alphabetically.

10.

Fill in the grid with the letters as specified, only using unique letters. For example, if we used the numbers one to ten as words, this would be:

O	N	E	T	W
H	R	F	U	I
V	S	X	G	A
B	C	D	J	K
L	M	P	Q	Y

Be careful – it's easy to duplicate a letter.

Level 5 – Music

1.

First fill in the symbols. Each row has one more loop in the same orientation as the cells above. Then fill in the corresponding letters. You'll have to work out the order, but they are written in an ordered sequence (with X and Z missing). Try guessing the most frequent letter.

2.

Just follow the instructions.

3.

The cheat Bach used was that in Germany, B flat (B♭) was called B, while B natural (without the flat) was called H. We're using this too. If you don't read music, the top line is F and you go down the alphabet alternating lines and spaces (so the space below the top line is E, etc.) When you get to A, next one down is G.

4.

In case you are struggling filling in the letters, the full keyboard is provided opposite. To decipher the message, where there are two possible values write one above the other – only one will make sense in context.

A C D F H I K M O P R T U W Y A B D F G I K M N P R S U W Y Z B D E G I K L N P Q S U W X Z B C E G I J

5.
Fill in the colours of the rainbow, then sort the songs by the rainbow colours. This will let you know which of the artists' initials you are looking for.

6.
If you aren't sure what the music notation means, you can hear these notes played by going to the Conundrum website www.ConundrumBook.com and clicking through to 'Help'. It's then a simple key cipher. As explained in the Cracker's Guide, this cryptogram uses the common approach of grouping letters in equal length blocks to avoid easy decryption from word lengths.

7.
It should be fairly easy to guess the missing word – which sounds like the letter you need.

8.
Try writing the song titles out in an equal-spaced font, omitting numbers, spacing and punctuation. The answer is hidden in there.

9.
Just do the sum with the symphony numbers (e.g. Bernstein's Kaddish symphony is his third symphony, so the number would be 3).

10.
The captured text shows how the cipher works. Each pair of treble and bass notes identifies a letter. (The wiggly vertical symbols are rests, indicating spaces.) If you aren't sure which note is which, these are the ones used:

Level 6 – Biology

1.
Pair off the plants and find the odd one out.

2.
DNA code comes in three-letter blocks, each of which produces an amino acid. These acids have long names, two-character names and single letter names. Replace each three-letter block with the appropriate acid name. Note: if you find a table with U in it as one of the bases, this is an RNA table – you need DNA codons. (There is no U or O available in the cipher, so V is substituted for U and O is omitted.)

3.
You need to get a feel for the approximate size of the human genome in number of base pairs.

4.
A proof reader might spot the message, a letter at a time.

5.
Paleoanthropologist Louis Leakey was involved in the early careers of three primatologists who became leaders in their fields. Jane Goodall studied chimpanzees, Dian Fossey studied gorillas and Birutė Galdikas studied …

6.
It's Class that's missing. But where does it go?

7.
The agent once observed that she thought a long animal name had to have more than four characters.

8.
We're looking for collective nouns – some animals have more than one, but the ones we're looking for here are all in common use.

9.
A surprising number are real, but not all of them.

10.
To read off the hidden information from one end of it, you need to 'fold' the message by chopping it into a different number of equal lines.

Level 7 – Toys and games

1.
Do you really need a cue? Has the puzzle snookered you?

2.
Assume that each point (the triangles) on the board is a letter. Look for a way to spell out a message bearing in mind the information given below the picture of the board. The order will alternate colours and have increasing numbers of pieces.

3.
Playing with trains?

4.
Not sure what this is about? You need to check, mate. Be careful though. The notation is not symmetrical.

5.
You are looking for some colourful characters' surnames from a game to match the underlined words (one underlined word is a homophone). Note the email insists on using the English game or you will go wrong.

6.
No need to worry about double word scores.

7.
Each row is a letter. Add the column values where there are pieces on that row to find which letter. Each column has a specific value, enabling a row to indicate any number between 1 and 255, but the spy is only using the first 26 numbers to indicate the letter.

8.
Sometimes what's important is not what's there, but what isn't.

9.
If you need help, ask Rich Uncle Pennybags.

10.
The numbers are binary. Start with the letter value of the number on the smallest doll to get the first letter. Then the smallest goes 'inside' the medium one so we need the result of applying what's on the middle doll to the smallest doll, using the logical operator OR. And so on. Logical operators, such as OR, AND, NOT and XOR, are used in computing and transform a binary number. So, for example, NOT transforms a 0 into a 1 and a 1 into a 0.

Level 8 – Astronomy

1.
Read up on astronomers and metals.

2.
Each of the letters in the sequences are either initial letters or classifications of some set of astronomical bodies. In the middle one, part of a much longer sequence is extracted: these four were the first to be discovered.

3.
The intensity of light drops off with the square of the distance. So to find the distance to the new star we need the square root of ($\text{Distance}_{\text{OLD}}^2 \times \text{Luminosity}_{\text{OLD}} / \text{Luminosity}_{\text{NEW}}$).

4.
Work out which letters are missing.

5.
Unlike Cavor, you won't encounter selenites.

6.
The metre is defined as the distance light travels in a certain time.

7.
First fill in the letters you can from the decrypted message. You should be able to fill in the remaining two letters by realising that the key is the answer to the spy's hint in stellar terms.

8.
There is a unique solution. Stars in a constellation are formally named by their position in a constellation (e.g. Beta Tauri). But many of the brightest also have more familiar 'proper names'.

9.
A regularly occurring astronomical event. The name of the puzzle might be a clue. Go for first sighting.

10.
While the key isn't the phrase, the kind of things in the phrase tells us what the key is.

Level 9 – Murder mystery

Check the room dimensions.

Level 10 – Politics

1.

The person enciphering the message wrote two characters per piece of strip on the scytale. So to decipher it you have to take every N letter pairs, where N is the number of sides of the scytale that were used. For example if N is 5 and the message is

THSANUSISCISGESIDEYTISWRNGSOALAMITFIFTE.
ESTEVEHE

you would read off the text using every 5th pair, repeating the original message until all characters are used:

THSANUSISCISGESIDEYTISWRNGSOALAMITFIFTE.EST
EVEHETHSANUSISCISGESIDEYTISWRNGSOALAMITFIFT
E.ESTEVEHETHSANUSISCISGESIDEYTISWRNGSOALAMI
TFIFTE.ESTEVEHE...

i.e. THISISAMESSAGEWRITTENUSING...

2.

Victorian values are implied.

3.

A simple key cipher.

4.

We need an address book.

5.

Note the spellings of the words may not be the same as the name – but they sound (approximately) correct.

6.
Think American.

7.
Although this may not remain the case, English was one of the procedural languages of the EU in 2019.

8.
The rule shows how the letters of the countries are interlaced – there is one country for each distinct letter in the rule. The pattern follows the way the letters in the word are repeated. If the word was ACCRA and you were told to ignore R, then the pattern would be ACCA. We call the first country A and the second C (just use the order the letters first appear in the rule – they don't have to be in alphabetic order). Then we would interlace letters of the two countries as follows:

ACCAACCAACCAACCA ...

9.
Down under.

10.
From Mary's cipher we have also used special symbols for the words *is*, *of*, *that*, *the*, *there* and *this*. The original cipher had several characters that were null – i.e. they were ignored, just used as padding to throw the reader off the scent. We have only used one such character (though it may appear several times). There was also a special character that doubled the character that came after it. So if the doubling character were % then %L would mean LL. As there was no W character, %U represents W. As there is no V character, U is used instead.

Level 11 – Food and drink

1.

At the end of the process, each bottle has the same volume of liquid as it started with.

2.

You could just try every combination. But to get there more quickly think of another way of ranking the drinks in ascending order.

3.

Operatic dame.

4.

What are there three of in the recipe? And the name of the dish we're making sounds rather like what we're counting.

5.

The 'parts' numbers point to a specific letter in a word.

6.

Forget the recipe, just look for patterns in the sequence of numbers.

7.

The section in capitals is the important part.

8.

Forget meanings: look at the letters. You are looking for something distinctive about all the other words that isn't true about the odd one out.

9.
The sentence 'Play fair with a testing typewriter sentence. I=J, you know' tells us to use the same character for I and J, which type of cipher this is, and which phrase is used to fill in the grid. That's a sentence traditionally used to test typewriters, as it contains all the letters of the alphabet.

10.
Each number derives from the numbers in one row of the typical values. Treat each digit in the row separately. Adding is required.

Level 12 – Mathematics

1.
Count the number of letters in each word of the poem.

2.
X and Y are the first and last names of this British philosopher/mathematician.

3.
Whole number complex numbers in the form a+ib can point to positions on a two-dimensional grid. This grid has been populated with letters in an orderly fashion.

4.
Note the first character in the sequence you must solve is a letter.

5.
It's a matter of matrix multiplication. Convert the letters to numbers first.

6.

Georg Cantor realised there was more than one size of infinity. The 'smallest' infinity is the infinity of the integers, which he gave a particular name.

7.

Draw a diagram with each of the fourteen possible first children (Boy Monday, Boy Tuesday ... Girl Sunday). Each connects to all fourteen possible second children (Boy Monday ... Girl Sunday). Pick out the number of combinations (Y) with a boy born on Tuesday and from these the number (X) where both are boys. The answer is X in Y – but be careful not to count the same combination twice.

8.

Column by column.

9.

Turn the percentages into real numbers to get to the details. For example how many people will be told they have the disease, but don't?

10.

Come up with a mathematical numerical constant which could be referred to as 'Eeh'. Use the numbers to decipher the cipher text. Then put the result into the grid in a systematic fashion – one arrangement will produce plain text if read in a different direction.

Level 13 – Sport

1.

One letter per team.

2.

Spot the balls.

3.

The first letter of a missing piece of information for each location.

4.

There is a quick way to work this out in your head, requiring only one addition, one division and one multiplication.

5.

A great circle is the minimum flight distance – the equivalent of a straight line on a curved surface.

6.

What is significant about them being home games?

7.

Think athletics.

8.

Not every entry is genuine.

9.

Make sure this a real person, not a fictional character.

10.

The letters at the bottom are a sequence not a cipher. Use them to pick a location, a number within that location and from that a letter.

Level 14 – Transport

1.
Think phonetic.

2.
You need first to re-encipher with MH before you decipher with the real key.

3.
States can have several different nicknames, but these have all been used.

4.
The Royal Mail's postcode finder is available on the Royal Mail website (or you can ask at a post office).

5.
Take a look at her baggage tags.

6.
You're looking for a road.

7.
Get yourself a London tube map.

8.
The outer line is a peripheral road and the inner line is a river.

9.
The key needs to be variable, so will only make use of the variable text on the boarding pass (large text in boxes).

10.
Think linearly.

Level 15 – TV

1.
Watch out for a balloon-like device named Rover.

2.
The key phrase already in the grid is the name of a company (at least, to start with) in a very popular TV series. Remember in these grids letters can't be duplicated, so the second part of the name is truncated.

3.
No further hints.

4.
Hawkins, Indiana is the fictional setting of *Stranger Things*, the Netflix show. The name of the alternate universe there should give a clue to handling Key 1.

5.
Make sure you give a collegiate answer.

6.
≈ means 'is approximately equal to'; ≡ means 'is identical to'.

7.
What's more, Mattie becomes Zoe and Tim becomes Doug.

8.
No hint.

9.
Napoleon and Ilya report to Alexander.

10.
For each letter after the first, Homer carries out the same operation. Work out how he got from HO to HW at the start of his name, and the rest will follow.

Level 16 onwards

You are on your own.